Science Smart Junior

with DVD

Discovering the Secrets of Science

by David Linker

Random House, Inc., New York
www.randomhouse.com

Editor: Russell Kahn
Director of Production: Iam Williams
Design Director: Tina McMaster
Art Director: Neil McMahon
Production Manager: Mike Rockwitz
Illustrator: Paulo De Freitas Jr.

ISBN: 0-375-76359-7
First Edition
Manufactured in the United States of America
10 9 8 7 6 5 4 3 2 1

ACKNOWLEDGMENTS

I would like to thank Reed Talada for indulging me when I asked for the time to write this book. Special thanks are also due to Russell Kahn, Scott Bridi, Kallie Shimek, Rachael Nevins, and Kristen Azzara for their unflagging editorial support, nutritional advice, and flexibility with schedules; to Paulo De Freitas Jr. for his expert artwork; and to Iam Williams, Tina McMaster, Michael Rockwitz, and Alexandra Morrill for their diligence, hard work, and attention to detail throughout. I'd also like to thank Ted Wallace for saving my dignity at the very last moment and Jodi Weiss for her constant support.

And lastly, I'd like to thank my wife, Jen, for never once doubting that I knew what I was doing.

CONTENTS

Introduction

A Very Sneaky Thing

We have done a terribly sneaky thing. In a zany story about four curious kids, a sleepy cat, and a flying dinosaur named Bob, we have hidden *science*.

Not Science!

Yes, science. But don't be afraid. Each chapter tells part of an adventure while covering different scientific facts and theories. You'll learn about everything from comets, chromosomes, and conduction to volcanoes, Venus, and velocity. Throughout the book, as you review and learn all sorts of crazy stuff, there are fun, safe experiments for you to try. The interactive experiments will help you better understand the science ideas. And if you have a problem with an experiment, don't sweat it. At the end of the book, there's a full answer key with easy-to-understand explanations. The great thing about this book is that it's yours, all yours. You can work at your own pace, redo experiments as many times as you'd like, or take a relaxing break before plowing on to the next chapter.

HOW TO PLOW

There are quizzes at the end of most chapters, and there is a glossary at the end of the book. The glossary will define all the science terms you've just read about. When a word is printed in extra-dark letters in the text (called **boldface**), that word is explained in the glossary.

SAFETY

Good science is safe science. We've tried to note when certain experiments are trickier or more potentially dangerous than others. However, every experiment should be conducted with the greatest care and precaution. Always wear safety goggles. Always have adult supervision. Always follow directions carefully. Performing experiments is a terrific opportunity to learn and make science fun, but every smart scientist knows that hurting yourself or damaging materials is not the way to find answers to anything.

Materials and Your Science Smart Journal

Most of the materials you'll need to do the experiments in this book will probably be around the house. However, it's a good idea to review a chapter first, see what you'll need to do the experiments in that chapter, and then check with an adult to make sure you have the materials that you need.

Also, throughout the book you'll be asked to make notes in your *Science Smart Journal*. Your *Science Smart Journal* can be a simple notebook. It's just a place where you have room to write notes, make predictions, sketch outcomes, design experiments, and chart results. Your *Science Smart Journal* is your own private science diary.

Part of being a scientist is learning to make educated guesses, testing your guesses, and then revising and revising and revising until you're right. You think Einstein came up with $E = MC^2$ on the first try? Not a chance. Science is all about being wrong sometimes, and your *Science Smart Journal* is your private place to be wrong until you can figure out how to be right!

A Note to Parents and Teachers

This book reviews the National Science Education Content Standards for grades 5–8. Interspersed within the story of the adventures of Beauregard, Barnaby, Angie, Babette, and Bridget are a number of do-it-yourself experiments. At the end of each chapter are review questions and exercises, and at the end of the book is a brief practice test to give students the chance to show what they know. The book should be used as a way to get students excited about science and to begin exploring ideas that they will return to in school.

As a teacher or parent, you should be prepared to supervise all experiments. (Even the simplest experiment is safest when conducted under the watchful eye of an adult.) Also, be prepared for questions about the material. This book is a primer, meant to introduce new ideas, and curious students will undoubtedly have questions that go beyond the scope of what we're able to review here. Push your students to ask questions about what they read and to make connections between the experiments conducted and the science learned.

Chapter 1

In the Beginning

It was all Barnaby's fault. Babette had come all the way from France to visit, and Barnaby had to baby-sit his kid sister, Angie. There was no wiggling out of it. Their Friday night was ruined. Bridget couldn't believe it when Barnaby told her over the phone that he couldn't make it. "Have fun at the Yankees game without me," he sighed heavily. "I'll be okay. At home. Taking care of Angie."

"Barnaby may be a genius scientist," Bridget thought, "but he's a really poor actor."

"Hold on," Bridget said, turning her Yankees cap backwards before pressing the phone to her chest. "Babette," Bridget said, "Barnaby can't make it to the Yankees game; we'll have to go without him."

"Poor Barnaby," Babette said, lowering her sunglasses to the edge of her nose. "Home baby-sitting on a Friday night. It is no fun. We should baby-sit with him."

"But . . . but . . ." Bridget stuttered. "I got us tickets right behind home plate. It's game four of the World Series. They could clinch."

"Clinch. Clatch. Clunch," Babette said with a wave of her hand. "Your good friend Barnaby, the most brilliant scientist since Madame Curie—may she rest in peace—needs our help. And you, you are worried about some silly football game."

"It's not football, it's baseball—and not just any baseball game," Bridget said in an angry whisper. "It's the Yankees, the New York Yankees. They're about to win the World Series! I've been waiting all year for this."

"So you will wait until another year. Barnaby needs us."

"I'll say," Bridget sighed, throwing up her hands.

"You'll say what?" Babette asked.

"It's an expression."

"How do you mean? I do not understand this American expression. You are a silly people with your footbase games and your pizza with toppings. I am curious to try one."

"Have you ever met Barnaby's kid sister, Angie?"

"He wrote me about her once. Or was that Beauregard the cat he spoke of? Who can remember such things?"

"If you think Barnaby is brilliant, then Angie is brilliant-squared," Bridget said, looking at the cat asleep on the windowsill. Beauregard raised his head, and then he rolled over and stretched in the setting sunshine.

"If she is so smart, then why does she need a baby-sitter? She can take care of herself, no? Tell Barnaby to pack his things. I want to go to this bingball game so you can buy me a hot dog. It seems cruel, but the dog is dead, no?"

"A hot dog isn't a real dog, and, much as I want to go, it's exactly because Angie is so brilliant that she needs, like, an army of baby-sitters."

"You joke, no?"

"No," Bridget said, shaking her head. "Not at all. She understands science as well as your Madame Curie did when she was eight years old. Angie just hasn't done all the experiments the rest of us have."

"I have done few experiments myself," responded Babette. "I find science fascinating."

"Yeah, but without trying it, you probably know that if you put a fishbowl in the freezer that the water will freeze, the bowl might crack, and the fish . . . " Bridget trailed off. "Those poor fish . . . "

"Yes. This I know. So?"

"So, imagine if every time you had a question, you put together your own experiment to figure out the answer."

"*Sacre bleu!* Barnaby," Babette said, snatching the phone away, "tell your horses they should hold on. We are coming right over."

✎   ✎   ✎   ✎   ✎

When Bridget, Babette, and Beauregard arrived at Barnaby and Angie's house, they heard the sound of glass shattering and then the pitter-patter of bare feet running away. Bridget had a pizza in hand (vegetarian—Barnaby's favorite), Babette had a French video, and Beauregard, well, he brought himself, which he figured should be more than enough. Barnaby threw open the front door. "You've got to help me," he said without so much as a hello. Barnaby looked as if he just stepped off an amusement park ride. His hair was a wild mess, and his lab coat was half-tucked into his jeans. He held out a dustpan with the shattered remains of what must have once been a serving platter. "You don't have any adhesives on you, do you?"

"Not unless you can use the cheese on this pizza," Bridget said. Barnaby looked over his shoulder before tossing the pieces into the shrubs.

"But Barnaby," Babette said, "what is wrong? We brought pizza and the greatest movie in the history of French cinema—*The 400 Blows* by Francois Truffaut. We'll watch it after the ball-and-base game."

"It's subtitled," Bridget cut in.

"Whatever!" Barnaby practically screamed. "Angie is on a tear."

"Did she . . . ?" Babette asked, nodding toward the shattered plate in the shrubs.

"That? No, that was my fault. We were discussing the difference between centripetal and centrifugal forces . . . . Let's just say that dinnerware doesn't fly well."

At that, Beauregard, who had fallen asleep on the welcome mat, got up and started to walk away. "Oh no you don't," Bridget said, grabbing him by the collar. "We're all in this together. Inside," she told Beauregard, and the three of them followed Barnaby into his living room.

Barnaby was pacing back and forth, hands over his head, as if he were trying to grab air. "The thing is, guys: I can't get her out of the bath."

"That is all?" Babette said. "No problem. We will be eating pizza in no time. You Americans do things strangely. I hear you eat this pizza entrée with your hands."

"You don't understand," Barnaby cut in rather abruptly. "She's trying to determine if she's soluble. She's drawn a fifty-gallon bath and she wants to see how long it will take for her to dissolve."

"Well, we better get her out of there before she does," Bridget said, hopping up the stairs two steps at a time.

"Wait, wait," Barnaby yelled before Bridget was barely halfway up, "she won't dissolve. People don't dissolve. Not in a tub of lukewarm water at least."

"Why not?" Babette asked. "Sometimes I come out of a bath and I feel like I've just drifted away."

"Different substances dissolve differently. She's fine for the moment. Let me show you something," Barnaby said, leading his friends to his downstairs lab. He handed them both goggles before taking out three glasses, a bottle of water, salt, sugar, rice and two stirring rods.

TRY IT YOURSELF!

Sugar and Salt

MATERIALS
600 ml of water, 3 equal-sized glasses,
4 tablespoons of sugar, 4 tablespoons of salt,
4 tablespoons of rice, 3 stirrers

STEPS
1. Put 200 ml of water in each of the three glasses.
2. Add 4 tablespoons of sugar to one glass, 4 tablespoons of rice to the second glass and 4 tablespoons of salt to the third glass.
3. Stir the glasses at the same rate for approximately 1 minute. Compare your results in your *Science Smart Journal*.

"See!" Barnaby said, holding up both mixtures to the light. "We've just demonstrated that both salt and sugar are soluble in water. We've made two mixtures: a mixture of salt and water and a mixture of sugar and water. A **mixture** is a combination of two or more substances in which the basic identity of the original substances is not changed!" Despite Barnaby's enthusiasm, his friends were unimpressed. Bridget and Babette both had their arms crossed, and Beauregard was asleep—again.

"What's the score of the Yankees game?" Bridget said then, heading upstairs to the television.

"For this," Babette said, sliding her glasses up on top of her head, "I let my first American pizza get cold?"

"You don't understand," Barnaby yelled after them. "Tell me this: What most affected the rates of solubility?"

Bridget and Babette stopped in their tracks and stared at each other. "How fast you stir the solutions?" Bridget asked tentatively.

"True, but take it one step further: Why does how fast I stir affect the rate of solubility?"

"Because, I think," Babette noted cautiously, "you are maybe adding motion?"

"*Precisely!*" Barnaby cried out. "Now, obviously no one is stirring Angie. So what else could she do to alter the experiment?"

"She could," Bridget cut in, "take a bath in a car!!"

Barnaby furrowed his brow at that suggestion. "Interesting deduction; if a car were moving, it still wouldn't alter the mixture—the water, I mean."

Beauregard then leapt onto the table, and from there he jumped at the refrigerator door, knocking it open. A waft of cold air blew past the girls. "Oh," they said in unison, "temperature!"

"Exactly," Barnaby said, closing the refrigerator door. "Thank you, Beauregard." Without even a meow, the cat laid down where he'd been before. "We don't have another minute to spare. We need to show her how temperature affects solubility before she thinks to try it out—on herself!"

Chapter 2
The Properties of Matter

Barnaby, Bridget, and Babette crowded into the upstairs bathroom with Angie, who was in the bathtub. Beauregard had no use for bathing and firmly believed that people smelled terrible whether they bathed or not, so he stood the farthest away. Angie, for her part, was as quiet and still as any eight-year-old has ever been. She was determined that nobody was going to affect the outcome of her experiment.

"Now you understand," Barnaby began in a his most professorial tone, "that there are three phases of matter: **solid, liquid,** and **gas.** They can each be defined in terms of **volume**—the amount of space taken up by an object. Solids have a definite shape and volume. Liquids have a definite volume and an indefinite shape. And gases—poor, poor gases—have nothing, no definite shape or volume."

"But my experiment is about solubility," Angie interrupted. Then she turned to Babette and asked, "Do you think I've started dissolving yet?"

"I think you should get out of the tub at once," Babette said.

"We have a pizza," Bridget cooed. "You can have a slice if you get out now."

"Is it vegetable?" Angie asked, eyes wide. "I'm a vegetarian."

"In fact, it is," Babette said, crossing her arms in a harrumph. "It is vegetable and it is quickly getting cold. Have you seen what happens to melted cheese when it gets cold? I think maybe it's not a solid, liquid, or a gas."

Barnaby had set up three cups on the edge of the counter. One was marked, "SOLIDS," one "LIQUIDS," and the last one "GASES." "Allow me first to demonstrate," he told them.

TRY IT YOURSELF!

The Phases of Matter

MATERIALS
3 paper cups, water, one marble, perfume,
3 squares of paper large enough to cover the
tops of the cups, 3 small bowls,
1 permanent marker

STEPS
1. Label one cup "Solids," one "Liquids," and
   one "Gases."
2. Place your marble in the "Solids" cup.
   Cover the top with paper.
3. Pour water in the "Liquids" cup until it is
   about half full. Cover the top with paper.
4. Add one drop of perfume to the "Gases"
   cup. Cover the top with paper.
5. Let stand for 5 minutes.
6. For each cup, remove the paper and pour
   the contents into a bowl.
7. Note any odor that may result.

"So you see," Barnaby explained, "because the marble is solid, it maintained its shape. The water, which is a liquid, took the shape of the cup first and then it spread out into the bowl. And the perfume evaporated—changing from a liquid to a gas—and floated away."

"And here I was thinking you smelled nice all of sudden," Bridget cracked.

"Now, Angie," Barnaby begged, "why do you want to dissolve?"

The question seemed to confuse Angie for a moment. "To see if it is possible," she told her brother. As soon as the words were out of her mouth, she felt silly. "I guess it's kinda dumb, eh?"

"Not at all. But you've forgotten an important variable in the experiment."

"I have? What?" she asked.

"If you get out of the tub and dry off, I'll show you downstairs in the lab."

        ✎ ✎ ✎ ✎ ✎

Bridget, Babette, Barnaby, and Beauregard were waiting in the basement when Angie came downstairs with her pajamas on and her head wrapped in a towel. "We are reheating the pizza as we speak," Babette said before Angie had even hopped off the bottom step.

"One–nothing," Bridget screamed, pulling a pair of headphones off her ears. "The Yankees are winning."

Beauregard raised his head, looked over at Bridget, and then rolled over and went back to sleep.

"Temperature," Angie declared without being asked. "That's what I forgot."

"Exactly," Barnaby said as he reached into the refrigerator to take out two bottles of soda. "Remember, **solubility** means the amount of a substance that will dissolve in 100 grams of a solution at a given temperature. The key phrase is 'at a given temperature.' Change the temperature, right, and you change the solubility. Check it out."

TRY IT YOURSELF!

Temperature, Gases, and Liquids

MATERIALS
2 bottles of the same brand and type of soda: 1 cold and 1 at room temperature, 2 balloons, a clock, heavy-duty tape

STEPS
1. Slowly open the cold bottle of soda.
2. Cover the top with one balloon. Tape the balloon on tightly.
3. Shake the drink. Be careful not to point the bottle at anyone!
4. Record what happens in your *Science Smart Journal.*
5. Repeat steps 1–4 with the warmer bottle.

"You see," Barnaby began, "every substance has certain properties. Some substances are soluble in water, like salt. Some aren't, like a human being. That's a good thing, too. Imagine what would happen if you were soluble and went out in the rain! By the way, can anyone tell me another property that we could use to tell saltwater from freshwater?"

"They taste different," Angie cut in, thrusting her arm in the air as if she were back in science class.

"That's one difference, sure," Barnaby said slowly.

"I will not swim in saltwater," Babette said defiantly. "It dries out my skin."

"But that's not a property of saltwater," Bridget added. "That's just you being a wimp."

"I am not a wimp," Babette says, flexing a muscle. "Feel that?" Bridget gave Babette's bicep a squeeze, and then Babette got down on a knee so that Angie could also check out her muscle. "See? Give me something heavy to lift. I will show you who is the wimp-o here."

"Precisely!" Barnaby exclaimed, confusing everyone momentarily. "Heaviness—or more exactly, **mass**—is a physical property of substances. Mass is the amount of matter in an object. I, for instance, have more mass than Angie."

"So, you are saying that my muscles have more mass than yours do?" Babette asked, unsure.

"Not exactly," Barnaby added, shaking his head, "but because you are stronger, you can certainly lift things with more mass."

"You go, girl," Bridget said to Babette as they high-fived each other.

"There's an old riddle," Barnaby noted then, cocking an eyebrow. "'Which weighs more: A pound of gold or a pound of feathers?'"

"Gold," Bridget answered quickly, "duh!"

"Babette?"

"Of course," she agreed, smiling, "that is a property of gold. It has more mass than feathers."

"Wrong and wrong," Angie told them both. "They both weigh the same—one pound."

"Precisely! But then would a feather and a block of gold weigh the same?" Barnaby asked his little sister.

"No," she answered slowly. "You'd need way more feathers to make up a pound than you would blocks of gold."

"Correct again," Barnaby told her, beaming proudly. "The difference is the **density.** That's the amount of mass an object has compared to its volume."

TRY IT YOURSELF!

The Density Test

MATERIALS

1 stick of butter, 1 thick chocolate bar, 1 sugar cube, 1 large bowl of water, napkins, 1 knife

STEPS

1. Create a chart in your *Science Smart Journal*. Your chart should look something like this:

	Butter cube	Chocolate cube	Sugar cube
Prediction			
Observation			

Give yourself more space to write in each of the boxes in the chart.

2. Unwrap the stick of butter and the chocolate bar.
3. Cut a piece of butter and a piece of chocolate that are both approximately the same size as the sugar cube.

continued on next page

continued from previous page

4. Note in your *Science Smart Journal* which object weighs the most: the chocolate cube, the sugar cube, or the butter cube. (Use a scale if you have one.) Predict what you think will happen if you drop them in the water. Write your predictions in your *Science Smart Journal.*

5. One at a time, drop the chocolate cube, butter cube, and the sugar cube into the water and record what you see in your *Science Smart Journal.*

6. Think about how each item behaved. In your *Science Smart Journal,* guess why each of these materials sank or floated.

"So all the blocks were the same size but different weights. It's a matter of the density of the object," Barnaby explained, pointing to the water bowl, "and whether it's more or less dense than water. If it's more dense . . . "

" . . . it'll sink," Angie cut in. "And if it's less, it'll float. We got it already."

"And," added Barnaby, "a substance's density changes when it changes states. The temperature at which a substance changes from liquid to gas is its **boiling point.** The **melting point** is the temperature at which a substance changes from a solid to a liquid."

"But not everything has a melting and a boiling point," Angie argued. "Only water."

"*Au contraire, mon amie*," Babette cut in. "Everything has both."

"That's correct," Barnaby added. "How'd you know that, Babette?"

"It is simple. My father always said my mother has a very low boiling point."

"Take a look at this," Barnaby said, pulling down a chart hanging over the refrigerator. "It's a list of the boiling points of some common **elements.** Elements are substances that cannot be broken down into simpler substances by ordinary physical or chemical means."

Substance	Melting Point, °C	Boiling Point, °C
Aluminum	660	2,467
Hydrogen	−259	−253
Oxygen	−218	−183
Titanium	1,675	3,260

"Now imagine we were on the planet Mercury," Barnaby continued, but Bridget interrupted him.

"Speaking of boiling points, what temperature would you say would be hot enough to boil pizza?" she asked.

"Interesting," Barnaby said as he started scribbling equations on a chalkboard. "It depends on a number of variables, I suppose."

Babette sniffed the air before turning to Bridget to ask, "Do you smell what I smell?" And in unison both girls yelled, "The pizza's burning!" and rushed upstairs to the kitchen. Bridget grabbed an oven mitt, turned the dials off, and threw open the oven door. Smoke billowed from inside, and the fire alarm began to bleat as Barnaby and Angie made their way upstairs. Beauregard took one step onto the landing and wisely retreated back to the safety of the basement.

Angie was dumbfounded. "What happened?" she asked, tugging at her brother's pants leg.

"We burnt the pizza," Barnaby explained. "This is why Mom and Dad told us to be careful if we needed to heat anything up."

Babette took an oven mitt and carefully slid the pizza out of the oven. "It is always sad to see food go to waste," she told everyone as she let their dinner drop into the garbage.

"This evening is a total wreck," Bridget said, shaking her head to fight off the tears. "I wanted to show you America, and all you've seen is the density of butter and burnt pizza."

"Oh, Bridget," Babette explained, "I didn't come to see America. I came to see you. And here I am seeing you. Look," she added, raising her sunglasses briefly, "it's you. What more could I want? So we've missed the silly beanball game and ruined the pizza. We're together again, so who cares?"

"Oh no. I completely forgot. Baseball!" Bridget screamed, snapping her headphones back on her head. "My poor Yankees: What's the score?"

"It may seem we've ruined dinner," Barnaby cut in then, "but I think we've actually just witnessed something pretty remarkable."

"Yes, yes, I know. Density. It is wonderful. You are dense; I am not. Move on already, Barnaby," Babette said.

"Tell me this, Angie, the pizza that we just burned: Is it still a pizza?" Angie was stumped for a moment, so Barnaby continued: "I mean, the pizza is made out of certain substances, right? After it burned, was it still made up of the same substances?"

"I don't think so," Angie said cautiously.

"Precisely! A chemical change has taken place. A **chemical change** is when a substance changes into a different substance with new characteristics. When you toast marshmallows, for instance, if you leave them in the fire too long, the outside burns and changes from sugar into, well, burnt yuck. That's a chemical change, and you can't reverse it. A **physical change** is different. What do you think a physical change is, Angie?"

"When the look of something changes, but the substance doesn't change. And the change *can* be reversed."

"Precisely. Now give me an example."

As Angie took a moment to think, Babette cut in to say, "The perfume. It changed from a liquid to a gas, but it still was perfume."

"Precisely again! Adding salt to water to create saltwater is another example of a physical change. So is melting an ice cube to get water. Both examples can be returned to their original states. While Bridget waits for the score, someone hand me some vinegar. Let's put on our safety goggles and try another quick experiment."

TRY IT YOURSELF!

Mixing Up the Medicine

MATERIALS
1 jar, baking soda, vinegar, safety goggles, paper towel

STEPS
1. Describe the properties of the baking soda and the vinegar in your *Science Smart Journal*.
2. Place the jar on a paper towel. Mix the baking soda and vinegar in the jar.
3. Examine the reaction and record your observations in your *Science Smart Journal*. Do you think the reaction was a physical or chemical change?

"That's an example of a chemical change," Barnaby added. "When we combined the baking soda and the vinegar, bubbles appeared, meaning a gas appeared. This gas is a new substance."

"The Yankees are down two to one now!" Bridget cried. "See, this is what happens when I'm not watching carefully."

"We should order another pizza," Angie said. "I'm hungry."

"Maybe this one a little more French," Babette asked. "How about with frog legs? Mmm . . . ."

"Blech," Bridget cut in. "You're kidding, I hope."

"You Americans do not appreciate frog legs. Okay. How about escargot? It is delicious, a delicacy in my country."

"What is escargot?" Angie asked cautiously.

"I think you call it snails. They are delightfully slimy. They slide right down your throat."

"We are not," Bridget interrupted, "having a pizza with snails or frog legs or any kind of gunk."

"Really," Barnaby said, opening the pantry door, "because I know a terrific recipe for gunk. How about this? Bridget you order a plain pizza while I show everyone else a quick experiment in chemical reactions. And then we can decide if we want a pizza with gunk or just a plain pizza."

TRY IT YOURSELF!

Gunk

MATERIALS
2 teaspoons liquid starch, 2 teaspoons school glue, 1 large square sheet of wax paper, food coloring

STEPS
1. Mix the starch, glue, and a few drops of food coloring on your wax sheet. Mix until they begin to congeal into something that starts to separate from the paper.
2. Allow the substance to sit for 5 minutes.
3. Roll the substance into a ball or knead it into a worm.
4. Play with the gunk. Drop it, roll it, let it sit, slowly pull it apart. Record your observations in your *Science Smart Journal*.

"You see," Barnaby explained. "It's another chemical reaction. How do we know that, Angie?"

"Because the new substance is chemically different than the substances that went into forming it," Angie said. "We can't change it back into the original substance."

"Enough of this waiting around," Bridget said, heading into the living room. "The *plain* pizza should be here soon, and I need to watch the game." Bridget turned on the television, and one by one, Barnaby, Babette, and even Beauregard came in to join her. The Yankees were down by one run with two outs in the third inning. Derek Jeter was up. If anyone could tie the game, he could. Bridget was tense with each pitch. Her eyes were shut, and she was gripping Babette's hand so tightly it began to hurt. Then there was a crack of the bat on the ball. Jeter hit it to deep center field. "The center fielder has his back to the wall," the announcer said. "He jumps and he catches it. That was a close call. If the wind wasn't blowing in, golly, that would have been a home run."

"Hey," Barnaby thought to ask, "has anyone seen Angie?"

The three of them looked at one another in terror. Barnaby shot a glance over to the corner by the front door. "Uh oh," he said, "she's got my baseball bat."

"She's started experimenting again," Bridget said, taking a peek out the back window. "The baseball game must have tipped her off on to motion and forces."

"What? It's just a game. There's no science to it."

"As Babette would say," Bridget quipped, "'*Au contraire.*' Baseball is all about unbalanced forces. Let me demonstrate quickly."

TRY IT YOURSELF!

The Unbalanced Bubble Meter

MATERIALS
1 empty soda bottle, paper, pen, tape,
and ruler

STEPS
1. Fill the bottle with water. When the bottle
   is capped and tipped on its side, you'll see
   a small bubble of air. (If you see more than
   one bubble, tap on the side of the bottle
   until you only have one bubble left.)
2. Cut a strip of paper about the size of a
   ruler. Draw marks either every half-inch or
   one centimeter apart. Now, tape the paper
   to the side of the bottle.
3. Lay your bottle on a flat surface. Pull it or
   push it at different speeds and record in
   your *Science Smart Journal* what happens to
   the bubble. Try pushing or pulling it at a
   constant speed. Record what you see.

"So you see," Barnaby explained, "the
bubble moves farther the faster and more jarringly
you pull or push the bottle."

"Just like a baseball flies farther the harder you
hit or throw it. That's cool," Bridget added.

"Yes, rather," Barnaby said, opening the
window shades, "until your little sister decides she
wants to see the effects of unbalanced forces on—no,

no, no—my science equipment!" Without another moment's hesitation the three kids raced out into the backyard.

☞ **QUIZ #1** ☜

Planet	Average Surface Temperature
Pluto	−223°C
Uranus	−216°C
Saturn	−176°C
Venus	459°C

Take a look at Barnaby's chart of melting points and boiling points on page 18. Use the information there, along with the chart above for some planets, to answer the questions 1, 2, and 3.

1. On which of the planets listed above would aluminum foil melt if it were sitting on the surface?
   A. Uranus
   B. Venus
   C. Uranus and Venus
   D. None of the above

2. Which of the following elements would get hot enough to boil on Pluto?
   A. Oxygen
   B. Hydrogen
   C. Oxygen and Hydrogen
   D. None of the above

continued on next page

— *continued from previous page* —

3. If there were oxygen on Uranus, what state would it be in?
   A. Solid
   B. Liquid
   C. Gas
   D. None of the above

4. Louis wonders if running a marathon causes a physical change to the treads of his running sneakers. What kind of test could Louis do to find out if the race caused any physical changes to the treads?
   A. Before and after the marathon, use a small, accurate ruler to measure the height of the treads.
   B. Before and after the marathon, take the temperature of the treads with a small thermometer.
   C. After the race, compare the color of his treads to the treads on a new pair of shoes.
   D. Keep track of the distance the shoes went on the marathon.

5. Which of the following is an example of a chemical change?
   A. Ice melting
   B. A bike rusting
   C. Water boiling
   D. Salt dissolving in water

Matching

Match each word below with its correct meaning on the next page.

1. Solubility   _____

2. Density   _____

3. Chemical change   _____

4. Physical change   _____

5. Element   _____

6. Boiling point   _____

7. Melting point   _____

8. Mass   _____

9. Mixture   _____

A. A substance that cannot be broken down into simpler substances
B. The amount of matter in an object
C. The temperature at which a substance changes from liquid to gas
D. A combination of two or more substances in which the basic identities of the original substances are not changed
E. When a substance changes into a different substance with new characteristics
F. When the physical properties of a substance change, but the identity of the substance does not.
G. The temperature at which a substance changes from a solid to a liquid
H. The amount of mass an object has compared to its volume
I. The amount of a substance that can dissolve in 100 g of solvent at a given temperature

Chapter 3

Motions and Forces

Bridget, Barnaby, and Babette sprinted out to the backyard. The sun was setting over the horizon, and Angie had Barnaby's baseball bat and a crate full of assorted microscopes, test tubes, forceps, old notebooks, and more. She'd already sent two pairs of sterilized tongs tumbling under a tree, and she was rummaging through the box for what to hit next when Babette grabbed the bat out of her hands.

"Hey, what gives?" Angie said, spinning around.

"What do you think you are?" Babette said. "A based-balls player or something? Some sort of Ed Williams?"

"That's Ted Williams," Bridget corrected. "And he played for the Red Sox, so I'd prefer if you didn't say his name in my presence."

"I read about him on the plane. He was the greatest hitter ever, no?"

"He was on the Red Sox—end of discussion."

"I do not understand you Americans. First you want to dissolve in bathtubs, then you hit things with a bat, and now you do not like this barnball player just because of the color of his socks. You are a funny people."

"Hey, at least I'm not ordering frogs on my pizza," Bridget snapped back.

"Ladies," Barnaby said, "please."

"Not frogs. Frog legs. They are tasty. As you Americans would say, 'Like chicken.'"

"Ribbit," Bridget croaked.

"At least I do not eat heated dogs for dinner."

"Please, let's not . . . " Barnaby continued, stepping between the two of them.

"I just wanted to understand why the baseball didn't fly out of the stadium!" Angie yelled, quieting the three friends.

"Is that all then?" Barnaby asked. "Well, it's really all just a matter of **motion,** which is when an object experiences a change in position, and **force,** which is when matter experiences a push or pull. Let me show you something," Barnaby added, reaching first into his pocket to pull out a sheet of paper and then into his wild hair to pull out a stray pencil.

TRY IT YOURSELF!

Describing Motion

MATERIALS
1 pencil, 1 blank sheet of paper from your
Science Smart Journal, a centimeter ruler

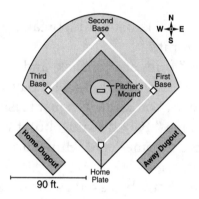

STEPS

1. Using the map above, what distance and in
   what direction must a baseball pitcher
   throw the ball if he were to throw the ball
   from the pitcher's mound to home plate?

2. What direction would a player go if she ran
   from second to third base and then to the
   home team dugout?

3. Where would a player end up if he ran
   approximately 120 feet north of home plate?

"You see, before you can talk about motion or force, you first have to understand **position,** which is where an object is in relation to a reference point. In this case, our reference point is either home plate or the dugout or such," Barnaby explained.

"Did you hear the doorbell?" Bridget asked abruptly, and all four children stood perfectly still for a moment to listen. And sure enough, the front bell rang again. "Pizza's here," Bridget said, "*sans* frog legs."

"Well then," Babette said, breaking a smile, "you can pay for it."

"Ribbit," Bridget shot back, and the bell rang again. "Fine," she said, sighing, "I'll pay. I guess I owe you anyway. You know I'm just teasing, right?"

"Of course," Babette said, "but it will not be so funny if the pizza comes cold. Hurry up." Bridget turned and ran off.

"Angie," Barnaby asked as the back screen door rattled shut behind Bridget, "now is as good a time as any to ask: Have you ever heard of **inertia**?"

"Inertia?" Angie said, placing a finger to her lips. "I don't think so."

"Tell me this: What's the hardest part of running?"

"Getting started!" Angie shouted.

"Precisely. Now do you know why that is?" he asked. When Angie shook her head, Barnaby answered his own question. "It's in large part because of inertia. Inertia is the tendency of an object to resist changes in motion. You know the difference between **velocity** and **acceleration,** right?"

"Velocity is the country where the Pope lives. It is in Italy, no?" Babette replied quickly.

"I think you're thinking of Vatican City," Barnaby answered slowly. "Velocity is how fast an object is moving in a given direction."

"And acceleration," Angie cut in, stealing the bat back from her brother, "is the change in either the velocity or the direction of travel of an object."

"Precisely!" Barnaby exclaimed proudly.

"So what does this have to do with inertia?" Angie asked.

"In a moment," Barnaby said. "First an experiment."

TRY IT YOURSELF!

A Penny Saved

MATERIALS
1 cup, 1 note card, 1 penny

STEPS
1. Put the note card over the cup.
2. Place the penny on top of the note card.
3. Pull the card away in a single, straight motion.
4. Record your observations and why you think it happened in your *Science Smart Journal.*

"So you see," Barnaby said, his hand stuck in the glass as he tried to get the penny out, "the card moves but the penny resists. It's inertia at its most beautiful."

And then, just as Barnaby popped his hand out, Bridget yelled, "Guys, come quick. I need help."

Babette, Angie, and Barnaby all turned quickly, jumped the three steps up the back porch, and ran across the living room to the front of the house. Even Beauregard was sufficiently curious to wake up and take a look. Bridget was desperately tugging at the front door, but it was stuck.

"You unlocked it?" Barnaby, ever the master of the obvious, asked.

"Yes," Bridget shot back. Just then the pizza guy peaked in the window, confused, gesturing that they should open the door so he could give them their pie.

"We are trying," Babette yelled back to explain, "but it is our personal Maginot Line. It seems it cannot be moved."

"What?" Bridget asked, pausing from her pulling.

"The Maginot Line. It was supposed to be France's defense against enemy invasion before World War II. But then the Germans, they just came right around it, and we couldn't defend ourselves because, like the door, everything was stuck in place," Babette explained.

"Ah, I see," Bridget said before adding, "Enough history. Help please." And the five of them lined up, each holding on to the other as if they were about to conga—Beauregard even helped by pulling on Angie's pants leg with his teeth—and on the count of three, they all pulled backwards. The door sprang open. Bridget fell on top of Babette who toppled onto Barnaby who nearly crushed Angie who missed Beauregard by inches. The delivery boy stood puzzled at the doorway, pizza box in hand.

"You ordered a pizza?" the pizza boy asked, his voice cracking.

"No toppings," Bridget said.

The pizza boy checked under the lid and said, "Uh oh."

"Uh oh?" Babette replied. "What is 'uh oh'? I do not understand this 'uh oh'. Is it American for 'yes we have your pizza'? Does it mean 'dinner is served' or 'have a good night'? I think it must, because here you are with the pizza we ordered. So, 'uh oh' to you too, sir. Thank you for bringing us our pizza so we might eat it and watch our thrilling battered balls game."

"It's a sausage, pepperoni, meatball, bacon, and ham pie—the meat lovers special," he said. Angie, Babette, Bridget, and Barnaby all groaned in unison. "You can pick it off, I guess," he said, showing them their pizza, which was almost completely covered in a variety of pork and beef.

"How long would it take you to go back and bring us a plain pizza?" Bridget asked.

"You don't want it?" he croaked.

"We have two vegetarians in our midst," Bridget explained.

"Oh," he told them, "I guess about half an hour." Across the doorjamb the kids all stood staring at one another before the pizza boy thought to say, "Oh, you want me to go *now*?"

"Please," Bridget said, "and if you could return with a plain pie as soon as possible, we'd really appreciate it."

"Right, one pizza and hold the meat. I'm on it," he said, saluting before walking back to his beat-up delivery car. Bridget closed the door carefully behind him.

"When he comes back," Barnaby added then, pulling a can of oil out of his pocket, "let's hope he holds the friction, too." Carefully he put a few drops of oil on the door hinges as Bridget and Babette both groaned at his attempt at a joke.

"What's **friction** got to do with it?" Angie asked.

"Friction is a force that resists motion between two objects that are in contact," Barnaby said. In this case, there was friction between the metal in the hinges and between the door and its frame."

"But why wasn't it inertia?" Angie whined. "I thought the door was resisting change."

"That's a very good question. But then why can I open the door now?" Barnaby asked, opening the door easily. "It's still the same door. It still has the same inertia. Only the amount of friction has changed. It's easy to confuse inertia and friction, but friction only acts on objects in contact—like the metal on the hinges of the door. Inertia acts on all objects. While we wait for the new pizza, why don't we try another experiment down in the basement?"

"But the game, the game," Bridget complained.

"Right, the game. If you want to stay to watch, this shouldn't take more than a few minutes," Barnaby said. "We're just going to have a little game of our own downstairs."

Bridget stared longingly at the television, sighed, and said, "Fine, I wouldn't want to miss out on the fun." She let her headphones clamp back onto her ears.

TRY IT YOURSELF!

Faster Friction

MATERIALS
4–6 sheets of paper towel, 1 hand towel, 60 cm
of aluminum foil, 60 cm of plastic wrap,
1 marble, a measuring tape, 2 rulers,
1 dictionary (or other thick book)

STEPS
1. Clear off a table or countertop. Make an inclined track by arranging each of the two rulers with one end on the dictionary and the other on the table next to each other. They should be close enough together so the marble doesn't fall between.
2. If you have more than one person participating, each of you should chose either the hand towel, aluminum foil, plastic wrap, or paper towel based on which you think will allow the marble to roll the farthest.
3. Lay the paper towel under the rulers and along the table or countertop. Choose a release point (an inch or a centimeter from the top of the rulers) and release. Don't push the marble from the starting point.

— *continued on next page* —

— continued from previous page —

4. Measure the distance from the bottom of your ruler "track" to where the marble stopped on the paper towel. Write the distance down in your *Science Smart Journal*. Try it three more times, each time recording the distance. Find the average (arithmetic mean) of the four trials.

5. Repeat steps 3 and 4 placing the hand towel, aluminum foil, or plastic wrap on the table.

6. Crumple the aluminum foil and plastic wrap. Moisten the hand towel and paper towel. Write down how you think this will affect your outcomes. Retest.

"So you see," Barnaby explained, "the marble traveled the shortest distance over the item that produced the greatest friction."

"So that's why the ball didn't leave the stadium," Angie exclaimed. "Friction!"

"In part," Barnaby said cautiously.

"How can there be friction," Bridget yelled— her headphones were still on. "The ball was in the air."

"Precisely!" Barnaby said.

"Precisely what?"

"The air. It creates friction too. Everything creates some friction. Even ice, which is slippery, exerts friction. Things eventually come to a stop, even when you slide them across ice. **Newton's first law of motion** states that bodies in motion remain in motion and that bodies at rest remain at rest unless acted on by an outside force, a push or pull. Friction is one example of a force. Without friction, a moving object would just keep moving forever. But friction doesn't explain the whole story."

"Well, of course, there is **gravity** at work, too," Babette chimed in. "It is a result of Newton's first law of getting conked on the head by an apple."

"Precisely!" Barnaby said. "Gravity is a remarkable thing, really. All objects pull on each other. For instance, Bridget, there is a gravitational attraction between you and me."

"You wish," Bridget quipped back.

"It's a fact. But because your mass and mine are so small, we don't feel the gravitational force between us. Earth, on the other hand, is so massive that it pulls small bodies toward itself. That's why apples fall down and, in part, why some baseballs don't make it out of the stadium. Allow me to demonstrate," Barnaby told them as he reached into his pocket.

TRY IT YOURSELF!

The Pull of Gravity

MATERIALS
1 length of string (about 6 inches long),
1 ruler, 1 paper clip

STEPS
1. Tie one end of the string to the center of the ruler.
2. Tie the paper clip to the other end of the string.
3. Hold the ruler perfectly horizontally. Observe the position of the paper clip and record your observations in your *Science Smart Journal.*
4. Tilt the ruler at various angles. Observe the effect the tilting has on the position of the paper clip. Record your observations in your *Science Smart Journal.*

"I don't understand," Angie said, "why gravity didn't cause the ball to travel straight down."

"Why it's all about **balanced** and **unbalanced forces,** my dear," Barnaby answered. "Balanced forces are equal forces that act on an object and cancel each other out. They're the reason gravity doesn't squash you. Your body exerts a balanced force upward against gravity. Unbalanced forces, on the other hand, are when there is a greater force acting on an object in some direction."

"The Yankees just took the lead!" Bridget yelled, jumping up and down. "Bernie Williams just hit one off the left field wall, scoring two runs."

"Excellent example, Bridget," Barnaby said. "When Bernie hit the ball, it was a perfect example of an unbalanced force. The bat exerted enough force on the ball to make it change direction completely. But now tell me this, Angie: When the ball hit the wall, why didn't it go right through the wall?"

Angie, by this point, was completely confused. "I like my experiment better," she said, and she turned to go back to the yard and take swings at the rest of the objects she'd collected.

"Answer this first," Barnaby cut in before Angie had even taken a step. "Say I fired a cannonball. Would it go through the wall?"

Angie stopped in her tracks to think about it, but before she could reach an answer, Babette cut in. "Of course it would," she said in her thick French accent. "Cannonballs are built to go through walls."

"Precisely!"

"But why?" Angie whined.

"What's the most obvious difference," Barnaby began, "between a cannonball and a baseball?"

"Well, a cannonball weighs more," Angie snapped.

"Precisely," Barnaby said again, smiling before crossing his arms.

"So the weight of something affects how much force it can exert," Angie said. "But then what if instead of firing the cannonball, I rolled it at the wall just using my hands. Would it still go through the wall?"

"Not unless you really got some muscle behind it," Bridget smirked. "Maybe if Babette rolled it."

"You are very sarcastic," Babette sighed.

"So the force an object can exert depends on its weight and its speed?" Angie asked slowly.

"Precisely," Barnaby said, throwing up his hands. "**Newton's second law of motion** states that the force acting on an object is equal to the mass of the object times the acceleration of the object (Force = Mass × Acceleration). So a baseball, because it has very little mass, would have to be accelerating quickly to have enough force to go through the wall on impact. However, a cannonball, because it has much more mass, doesn't need to travel nearly as fast to exert enough force to go through the wall. Allow me to demonstrate."

TRY IT YOURSELF!

The Distance Race

MATERIALS
2 cans (one empty, one full), 2 books, 1 thin piece of wood about 12 inches long, 1 pen, a measuring tape

STEPS
1. Place both books on top of each other. Place one end of the wood on top of the stacked books and the other end of wood on the floor to create a ramp.
2. Mark a point on the wood as your starting line.
3. Place the full can on the starting line. Without pushing it, release the can down the ramp.
4. Measure how far the can travels.
5. Repeat steps 3 and 4 with the empty can.
6. In your *Science Smart Journal,* write down what you observe and why you think one rolled farther than the other.
7. You can repeat the experiment with other cans. First, compare their weight to original cans, predict how far each will travel in comparison to each other, and then let the races begin.

"See, the can with the greatest mass took the longest to slow down. This is why it traveled the farthest," explained Barnaby. " The more mass an object has, the harder it is to change its motion. That's why it's harder to slow a bus down than a tricycle."

And on that, they all tromped off to the living room. Bridget flicked on the television. It was only the third inning. The Yankees were still winning. All was good in the world for the moment. Even Beauregard had found a comfortable spot to nap on the windowsill. He looked as exhausted as any cat ever has.

Outside, the world had slowed. The last hints of daylight colored the evening, and the moon was already visible against the purple, cloud-veined skies. "I am starving," Babette said, clutching her stomach as she slumped into the recliner chair. "Where is that pizza? Is there no café we can go to where we can at least get a croissant or baguette to tide us over?"

"We have some ice cream in the freezer," Barnaby said. "Angie, can you grab us some?" When she didn't respond, Barnaby asked again, "Angie?" And then he became nervous. "Ang?" he called out using the nickname their mother gave her. "Where's Angie?" he asked Bridget and Babette.

"I saw her go outside," Bridget said, distractedly. "Something about the tree house and her trampoline."

"The tree house and her trampoline?" Barnaby asked. "She wouldn't . . . " he began. "No, she's smarter than that. Of course, of course," and before the words were out of his mouth, he was already out of his seat.

"What now?" Bridget said.

"She's figured out the next step," Barnaby said.

"Next step? I do not understand. What is the next step?" Babette yelled after him as she reluctantly followed him outside again.

"Work," Barnaby explained with a gulp, "equals force times, oh goodness," he added as he got out onto the front steps and spun around to see his sister climbing up into their tree house, "distance!"

DESIGN IT YOURSELF!

Directions: Barnaby explained the difference between a balanced and unbalanced force on pages 43–44. Your task is to come up with an experiment that demonstrates the difference between the two. Fill in the details and the steps in your *Science Smart Journal.*

Experiment Title?

_____

MATERIALS

_____
_____
_____

STEPS

_____
_____
_____
_____
_____
_____

continued on next page

continued from previous page

Before you do your experiment, what is your prediction for the results?

_____

_____

_____

_____

_____

_____

What results did you get?

_____

_____

_____

_____

_____

If your results are different from what you predicted, explain why.

_____

_____

_____

_____

_____

✍ QUIZ #4 ✍
Matching

Match each word in the column below with its correct meaning on the next page.

1. Inertia   _____

2. Unbalanced forces   _____

3. Friction   _____

4. Newton's second law of motion   _____

5. Balanced forces   _____

6. Force   _____

7. Gravity   _____

8. Acceleration   _____

9. Newton's first law of motion   _____

10. Motion   _____

11. Velocity   _____

12. Position   _____

A. A change in position of an object
B. A push or pull on matter
C. The tendency of an object to resist changes in motion
D. The speed an object is moving in a given direction
E. A change in either the velocity or the direction of travel of an object
F. A force that resists motion between two objects that are in contact
G. Bodies in motion remain in motion and bodies at rest remain at rest unless acted on by an outside force
H. The force that pulls all objects together
I. Equal forces that act on an object and cancel each other out
J. Forces acting on an object unequally in some directions
K. The force acting on an object is equal to the mass of the object times the acceleration of the object
L. Where an object is in relation to a reference point

Chapter 4
Energy

Barnaby, Bridget, and Babette stood out on the front yard, waving their hands in the air, yelling at Angie to please be careful. "The first rule of any scientific experiment," Barnaby told his little sister, "is to make sure that your experiment is safe. Angie, this is *not* a safe experiment."

"But," Angie argued, "if force equals mass times acceleration then if I can get enough mass and enough acceleration, I should be able to create a force great enough to launch me into space. How cool would that be?"

"Well, you've got one major flaw in your experiment, though," Barnaby told her calmly.

"What?"

"Come down and I'll tell you."

Defeated, shoulders hung, realizing then that if she missed the trampoline she'd be doing an experiment in broken ankles more than anything else, Angie relented. She slowly, carefully made her way back down the tree. Cheering, Babette and Bridget ran to meet Angie and Barnaby at the foot of the treehouse stairs. "That was a pretty close call," Bridget said, ruffling Angie's hair.

"You could have really hurt yourself," Babette said. "I was so worried that I forgot how hungry I am."

"Sorry," Angie said, looking up, her eyes moist. "I just thought that if I could get the trampoline to exert enough force on me, I could trampoline myself pretty far."

"Pretty far?" Barnaby said, laughing. "Angie wanted to put herself into orbit." And even Angie couldn't help but laugh at the thought of her circling the globe like a satellite with pigtails.

"So what was I doing wrong, big brother?" Angie asked.

"Tell me this: Why were you holding the dumbbells?" he asked.

"More mass," Angie answered quickly.

"She'll accelerate faster," Bridget cut in.

"Hold on, hold on. If you have more mass, what else do you have?" Barnaby asked.

"More inertia?" Angie squinted to ask.

"*Precisely!*"

"That is correct," Babette told them. "On the plane, I read about Galileo's early experiments with gravity. He proved that everything falls to Earth at the same speed, regardless of its weight."

"What were you reading on the airplane—the encyclopedia?" Bridget asked.

"It was a long flight," Babette said, shrugging.

"That can't be right, though," Angie cut in.

"No, it was a very, very long flight, and my leg room, it was cramped."

"I mean," Angie insisted, "if gravity works the same on all objects regardless of weight, why is it easier for me to lift a box up onto the first shelf, say, than it is for me to lift a box onto the top shelf?"

"Now, now, little sister," Barnaby warned, "you have to distinguish force from **work.** Work is energy transferred through both force and motion. We know that force equals mass times acceleration. Well, work equals force times distance, and force is given in units called **newtons**—named for Sir Isaac Newton, that squirrelly little genius."

"Don't forget,"added Barnaby without even giving his sister a moment to respond, "**energy** is the ability to do work or to produce change. It can be in the form of heat energy, light energy, sound energy, chemical energy, or electrical energy."

"But then, I'm confused," Angie said, scrunching up her face. "Force, work, and energy are all basically the same thing, aren't they?"

"A fine question," Barnaby said patiently, "but first an experiment."

TRY IT YOURSELF!

Catch!

MATERIALS
2 cups dry rice, 1 sock, 1 measuring cup, pen or pencil, yardstick, scale that measures grams, a helper.

STEPS
1. Pour the rice into the sock. Tie the sock.
2. Measure the mass of the rice on the scale.
3. Gravity has a constant acceleration of 9.8 m/s^2. Convert the weight of the sock from grams to kilograms (1 kg = 1,000 g). Use a calculator and determine the force gravity is exerting on the sock (Force = Mass (kg) × Acceleration (m/s^2). Write your answer in your *Science Smart Journal*.
4. Now lift the sock to a height of 1 yard. Calculate the work needed to do this (Work = Force × Distance).
5. Ask a helper to put his or her hand under the sock as close to the floor as possible without touching the floor. Drop the sock.

continued on next page

continued from previous page

6. Repeat steps 4 and 5 from a height of 1 meter. Ask your helper what he or she observed about the difference between a sock dropped from a height of 0.5 meters and a sock dropped from a height of 1 meter. Record his or her observations in your *Science Smart Journal*.

"When the sock is moving it has a special kind of energy—**kinetic energy**," Barnaby said. "That is, it has the energy of motion. Kinetic energy is equal to one-half the mass (in kilograms) times the velocity (in meters-per-second) squared—$E_k = \frac{1}{2}mv^2$. So how much *kinetic* energy an object has depends on its mass and on how fast it is moving. Both energy and work are given in units called **joules.** One joule is equal to the work done when a force of one newton acts over a distance of one meter."

"Okay, so then force is a push or pull of something, right?" Angie asked. To which, Barnaby just nodded. "So, it's what you need to do work. And the force on the sock is the same the whole way as you're picking it up, right?" Barnaby nodded again. "But work depends on how far you're moving something with that force. Which makes sense. It takes the same constant force to lift the sock 1 meter or 100 meters, but it's a lot harder to lift anything 100 meters."

"Precisely!" Barnaby exclaimed.

"You're making this all up," Bridget said. "Kinetic phooey. Things have energy because we give them energy. A ball is just a ball until a pitcher throws it."

"To borrow a phrase from Babette, '*Au contraire*,'" Barnaby told her. "You've forgotten about **potential energy**—or stored energy."

TRY IT YOURSELF

Hidden Potential

MATERIALS
1 bucket loosely filled with soil,
1 stake, 1 softball

STEPS
1. Press the stake about halfway into the bucket of dirt.
2. Hold the softball in your hand above the stake.
3. Drop the ball onto the stake. In your *Science Smart Journal*, record what happens.
4. Repeat steps 2 and 3.
5. In your *Science Smart Journal*, explain where the energy to drive the stake into the dirt came from.

"So what does that prove?" Bridget asked.

"Why, everything," Barnaby answered, surprised by Bridget's forcefulness. "Tell me this: Why does the ball eventually come to a rest?"

"Because, I think, it has used up its energy," Babette said.

"Precisely, but then why does it drive the stake farther down when we drop it again?"

"Because every time we pick the ball up, we add more energy into the system!" Angie exclaimed.

"So then does the ball have energy when we hold it above the stake?"

"Yes," Bridget answered, "it has potential energy. It's the energy we've added that we haven't used."

"And, and, and," Angie shouted, all excited, "the potential energy should be equal to the work we've just done lifting the ball."

"*Precisely!*" Barnaby said, beaming. "Remember work is equal to force times distance? Well, gravitational potential energy is equal to work times the height of the object ($E_p = W \times h$). Work and gravitational potential energy are directly related," he practically sang. "We apply a force on the ball and do work as we lift it up. While we hold the ball over the stake, it has potential energy. As the ball falls, it uses that potential energy and gets kinetic energy. When it stops moving, it has used up the energy we gave it by lifting it in the first place."

Babette groaned then, "Boring! Let's watch the movie or the bats and balls or something, please."

Being that Babette hadn't eaten and was a bit jet-lagged, she could feel the grumpies, as she called them, starting to set up camp. Bridget turned on the game, and the score was tied again.

"Well, I'll tell you one thing," Bridget sighed, plopping herself onto the couch, "the energy's sure been sucked out of this evening."

"We used up all our potential energy, I suppose," Angie said, yawning.

"Untrue," Barnaby said. "Energy cannot be created or destroyed. It's the **law of the conservation** of energy."

"Well, I'm pooped," Babette said. "I don't have the energy for another silly experiment."

"Then Bridget and Angie," Barnaby began, "why don't you help me this time?"

TRY IT YOURSELF!

The Conservation of Dizziness

MATERIALS
1 plastic lid, 4 feet of string

STEPS
1. Make two holes about a quarter of an inch apart in the plastic lid.
2. Run the string through the holes in the lid. Tie the ends of the string in a knot once it's through the holes.

— continued on next page —

continued from previous page

3. Hold the string at the two ends on either side of the lid and slide the lid to the middle of the looped string. Make sure the string is taut.

4. Rotate the lid in one direction until the string is wound. Release the lid. Observe both the string and the lid in motion. Record your observations in your *Science Smart Journal*.

"But the spinning stopped," Angie complained as she wound the lid to try again.

"Well answer me this: What else is acting on the string besides the energy that we gave it?" Barnaby said. "Think of our doorjamb conundrum."

"Friction," Angie said, smiling and nodding. "I get it."

"Exactly," Barnaby said. "Friction converts our mechanical energy into other forms of energy."

"Other forms of energy," Bridget sighed, flopping her head back, feigning exhaustion. "I don't think I can take another form of energy."

"Well, all types of energy are really either kinetic or potential, but they can be broken down into thermal, nuclear, chemical, and electrical, to name a few types. In this case, friction turned some of the potential energy into **heat,** which is thermal energy that is transfered from something of higher temperature—the string—to something of lower temperature—the air—you see."

"Just like with our pizza?" Angie chimed in.

"Our pizza," Bridget told her, "just got ruined. Look, I'm tired of waiting, and I'm tired of being hungry. I'm going to heat up some frozen burritos to tide me over. Anyone want one?"

"Frozen burritos?" Babette asked, wandering downstairs to join them.

"Frozen burritos are an American delicacy," Bridget told her friend. "They are in a food group called microwavable foods."

"Which provide an excellent example of conduction, and that's exactly what I'm talking about," Barnaby proclaimed.

"Can we not talk about science for one minute?" Bridget whined.

"How can we not talk about science?" Barnaby said. "Everything is science. When the pizza cooled down and when you microwave your frozen burritos . . . they're both examples of **conduction.** Conduction is when heat moves through a material or from one material to another. In our case, the heat moved from the pizza to the air until we reached a state of **thermal equilibrium**—that's a state of balance that occurs when two objects come in contact and the temperature of one becomes the same as the temperature of the other."

"Hey, how about an experiment," Bridget said, faking excitement.

"Yeah!" Angie said, jumping up and down.

"Now that's more like it," Barnaby added, smiling.

TRY IT YOURSELF!

Hot, Hot, Hot

MATERIALS
1 metal fork, 1 plastic fork, 1 wooden spoon, a small empty pot, a pot with 3 cups of hot water, 1 stick of butter, 3 small buttons

STEPS
1. Using a dab of butter, stick one button to the back of the forks and the spoon.
2. Stand the forks and the spoon in the small pot so that the buttons are hanging over the edge. If the butter melts, the buttons will fall. In your *Science Smart Journal* predict which button will fall first and why.
3. Pour the hot water from the pot into the small pot. In your *Science Smart Journal* note which button falls first. If your observations don't agree with your predictions, explain why.

"See, the heat flows up the spoons and melts the butter," Barnaby explained. "It's conduction at its best."

Just then the microwave finished heating their burritos. Bridget carefully took all four out and put them on paper plates for everyone. "Finally," she said, "sustenance."

Babette, being the most refined of the children, took a knife and a fork. She carefully sliced opened her cheese-and-broccoli burrito, and steam wafted up and fogged her glasses. "Now, look at that," she said, laughing, "conduction at work."

"Close," Barnaby said, "but no cigar."

"No cigar?" Babette said, wiping her glasses dry with a napkin. "Good, I do not like cigars anyway. They are stinky. Barnaby, I would have thought you knew better. They are very, very bad for you, too."

"It's an expression," Bridget explained wearily. "It means you almost got it right but you didn't."

"Well, I would not want to be right if being right means I have to smoke a stinky cigar."

"It's **convection**," Barnaby explained, "not conduction that caused your glasses to fog. Convection is a heat transfer by the motion of a heat-carrying medium—in this case, air."

TRY IT YOURSELF!

Spin, Spin, Spin

MATERIALS
1 note card, pen, scissors, 50 cm string, table lamp

STEPS
1. Trace a circle on your note card and then cut out the circle using the scissors. Fold the circle in half. Unfold. Then fold it in half the other direction. Repeat two more times so that you've got four equal creases—like a pizza pie.
2. Cut a notch about 1–2 cm long on each crease. Fold the right side of each notch down and the left side up so that it looks like this:

continued on next page

— continued from previous page —

3. Using your pen, poke a hole in the center of the circle. Pull your string through the hole and tie a small knot at the end. Your circle should hang from the string parallel to the ground.

4. Choose a lamp away from drafts. Have a parent or adult check the bulb to make sure that it's off and cool. Hold the circle by the end of the string about 10–20 cm above the lamp bulb. Stand as still as you can until the circle stops moving completely.

5. Ask a parent or adult to turn on the lamp. Watch your circle carefully. In your *Science Smart Journal* write down what you observe and the reasons you think the circle behaves this way.

"So you see, the heat from the bulb warms the air, which makes it less dense, so it flows upwards, and spins the circle," Barnaby said as if it were obvious. "Your glasses fogged because the moist air in the burrito convected upward, you see."

"And that," Angie concluded, "is also how we get heat from the sun."

"Whoa," Barnaby said throwing up his hands like a crossing guard would, "slow down there. Answer me this: Is there any air out in space?"

"No, that is why astronauts need helmets," Babette answered, taking a first cautionary bite of her burrito.

"Precisely. Remember convection is the movement of thermal energy by matter. In space, there is very, very little matter. **Radiation,** on the other hand, is the process through which thermal energy travels across a space. When we put the pizza in the oven to heat it up, that's radiation at work. You don't need any intermediate matter to transfer your thermal energy."

"So you're saying the sun just kind of dumps energy on us?" Bridget sighed.

"In a way," Barnaby said. "The radiation from the sun is what warms Earth. The energy comes in the form of light. Light travels in straight lines, and, for your information, it travels through some substances like space and air faster than it travels through others like water. Check this out."

TRY IT YOURSELF!

It's a Refract, Jack

MATERIALS
1 pencil, 1 glass, water

STEPS
1. Fill the glass halfway up with water.
2. Place the pencil in the water.
3. Stand directly over the water and look closely at the spot where the pencil leaves the water. Record your observations in your *Science Smart Journal.*
4. Move the pencil up and down and continue to observe the pencil closely. Describe in your *Science Smart Journal* what you see.

"What you see is called **refraction,** which is the process in which light bends when it passes from one substance to another," Barnaby explained, pulling a pad of paper from his pocket and another pencil out of his wild hair.

"But I thought you said light travels straight," Bridget mumbled, her mouth full.

"So I did. So I did. And I was right. See," he said, producing a quick sketch. "This is what happened."

"But, of course, light doesn't always refract," Angie said. "Sometimes it reflects too."

"Yes," he said, "but there are actually two kinds of reflection. **Regular reflection** occurs when light bounces right back at its source off a smooth surface. **Diffuse reflection** is when light bounces in many different directions, as off, say, aluminum foil or the page of a book."

"So light is always reflected or refracted," Angie said, nodding. "That's pretty cool, older brother."

"Except it's not *always* true."

"See," Bridget piped up, "I knew you were making all this science hoo-ha up."

"Sometimes," Barnaby said, "light can be absorbed too."

And just as Barnaby said that, there was a snapping sound and all the lights in the house went off. "Nice trick, Barnaby," Bridget said. "Now turn the lights back on."

"But, but," Barnaby stuttered, "I didn't turn the lights off."

"This is not funny, Barnaby," Bridget said. "You are scaring your sister."

"The electricity must be off," Barnaby said, swallowing. "Oh, dear."

Just then there was a thud from the side of the house. Barnaby screamed, terrified, and Bridget rushed over to quiet him. The four children huddled together. Only Beauregard seemed unafraid. He merely rolled over as if he wished someone would scratch his belly. It was completely dark outside. "I've heard ghost stories," Angie said.

"I don't believe in . . ." Barnaby began, until he heard another thud and a pained howl. "Oh, dear."

"They say it's the Ice Scream Man," Angie said. "He used to drive his truck around here every summer, remember?"

"And then," Barnaby said with a gulp, "he just stopped."

"That's right," Angie said, "they say his truck broke down, his ice cream melted, and so did he!" At that moment they heard a relentless pounding on the front door—boom, boom, boom! Barnaby ran up the stairs to his bedroom, and at once, Angie, Bridget, and Babette followed in a sprint.

"You kids better let me in," the voice cried from behind the front door as the four friends hid under Barnaby's bed. There was no need to experiment. It was a proven fact—they were all terrified.

≤ **QUIZ #5** ≥

DESIGN IT YOURSELF!

Directions: On page 69, before the lights went out, Barnaby began explaining what happens when light is absorbed. Objects that block the passage of light are called **opaque,** objects that let some light through are called **translucent,** and objects that let all light through are called **transparent.** Your task is to come up with an experiment that tests different objects to see if they are opaque, translucent, or transparent. (Make sure an adult checks your idea before you try your experiment.) Fill in the details and the steps in your *Science Smart Journal.*

— *continued on next page* —

continued from previous page

Experiment Title

_____

MATERIALS

_____

_____

_____

STEPS

_____

_____

_____

_____

_____

_____

Before you do your experiment, what is your prediction for the results?

_____

_____

What results did you get?

_____

_____

If your results are different from what you predicted, explain why.

_____

_____

_____

1. What is the mass of an object, if a force of 10 newtons gives it an acceleration of 5 m/s^2?
   A. 50 kg
   B. 15 kg
   C. 2 kg
   D. 2,000 kg

2. Donna must help her parents move. She packed some boxes so that they each have a mass of 15 kg. If Donna's mother has asked her to put these boxes on a table that is 2 meters tall, how much work does Donna have to do lifting each box?
   A. 30 joules
   B. 17 joules
   C. 7.5 joules
   D. 3 joules

3. Donna's family has a lot to move, so her mother stacks the boxes on top of each other to save space. Donna's mother has stacked two boxes, one on top of the other, on the table. The total mass of the boxes together is 30 kg and their height above the floor is 2 meters. How much potential energy do those two boxes have?

   A. 90 joules
   B. 60 joules
   C. 30 joules
   D. 15 joules

4. The boxes tumble off the table when the family's dog Lucky bumps into it. Together the boxes have a mass of 30 kg and they hit the floor at a speed of 3 m/s. What is the total kinetic energy produced by the fall?

   A. 32 joules
   B. 90 joules
   C. 110 joules
   D. 135 joules

✍ QUIZ #7 ✍
Matching

Match each word in the column with its correct meaning on the next page.

1. Regular reflection   _____

2. Thermal equilibrium   _____

3. Convection   _____

4. Heat   _____

5. Newton   _____

6. Kinetic energy   _____

7. Diffuse reflection   _____

8. Radiation   _____

9. Law of conservation of energy   _____

10. Conduction   _____

11. Refraction   _____

12. Work   _____

13. Potential energy   _____

14. Joule   _____

A. Occurs when light bounces right back at its original source
B. A state of balance that occurs when two objects come in contact and the temperature of one becomes the same as the temperature of the other
C. The energy of motion
D. A unit of force
E. The process in which light bends when it passes from one substance to another
F. When heat moves through a material or from one material to another
G. Thermal energy that is transferred from something of higher temperature to something of lower temperature
H. Energy can't be created or destroyed
I. A unit of energy or work
J. A heat transfer by the motion of a heat-carrying medium
K. Energy transferred through force and motion
L. Stored energy
M. The process through which thermal energy travels across a space
N. When light bounces in many different directions

Chapter 5
Living Systems

"It's the Ice Scream Man, for sure," Angie said, trembling under the bed. "We're all doomed." There was another loud rap at the door, and Angie, Barnaby, Babette, and Bridget all huddled closer together. Beauregard meowed loudly as if to let the kids know they were protected. In the dark, Barnaby's toys—his chemistry sets and dissection kits—all took on strange shapes. Everything looked like ghosts in the shadows. "I heard about this one family," Angie continued, swallowing hard, "that he ate. He put chocolate syrup on them all and ate them. That's what ghosts do."

"It can't be. It just can't," Barnaby said, shaking his head in disbelief. "Ghosts don't exist."

77

"Don't tempt him," Bridget shot back. "Ghosts hate it most when you think they don't exist."

"My parents have a chateau in Switzerland that is haunted," Babette confessed. "At night, when we stay there, I can hear the ghosts moaning."

And then from downstairs, there was a loud, low, "Ahhhhh." It sounded almost pained.

"And that's just what they sound like," Babette added, quivering.

"This is ridiculous," Barnaby said, getting out from under the bed.

"Barnaby, don't," his sister cried.

"I demand to meet this ghost," he said, picking up a microscope for a weapon.

"I will not let you go alone," Babette said, crawling out behind him. "All for one, as we say in my country, one for all."

"I don't know," Angie said, gathering up all her courage in one swallow as she stood.

"I'm staying right here," Bridget said, turning her cap around to hide under the brim. "I'll guard under the bed."

"Have it your way," Barnaby said. "If we don't make it back . . ." he began but then stopped in mid-thought, gathered his nerve, and marched downstairs. Babette and Angie followed right behind. Alone, hiding under the bed, Bridget sensed that the strange shadows were closing in. Each had gnarled hands and pointy fangs. It only took a moment alone for Bridget to decide to sprint down the stairs after her friends.

Babette was already tugging at the front door. Barnaby had his microscope up over his head ready to strike whomever might be there. Even little Angie had her fists bared, ready for a fight. On the third tug, the front door yanked open. Barnaby took a step forward, and the pizza delivery boy stood there dumbfounded. "Dudes," he said, nonplussed, "I burnt my finger on your doorbell."

"Pizza?" Bridget said, laughing hysterically. "Just pizza?"

"It's a plain pie this time. I checked it myself," he told them proudly.

"So you're not the Ice Scream Man?" asked Bridget, still shaking a bit.

"No way, I did that one summer. Lousy job. Your hands get all sticky. The real money's in pizza delivery. It's a growing business," he added, patting his stomach.

"When he rang the doorbell, he must have shorted the lights out," Barnaby explained. "It happens all the time." Barnaby flipped open the fuse box near the hall closet, flipped a switch twice, and the lights flickered back on.

"You are a strange group of little dudes," the pizza boy said as he gave Babette change for their pizza. "Have a good evening," he said, pausing to fake a ghostly laugh, "if you can."

"You see," Barnaby said, letting the door slam shut, "there's no such thing as ghosts."

"How can you be so sure?" Bridget asked, her hands on her hips.

"Because any thing that could walk around and ring doorbells must be made up of cells, and ghosts obviously don't have any," Barnaby explained with a sigh. "A **cell** is the basic unit of all living things. Let's try a quick experiment while we eat."

TRY IT YOURSELF!

A Yeasty Mess

MATERIALS
1 package dry yeast, sugar, warm tap water, microscope, 3 microscope slides, 2 bowls, 3 microscope slide covers

STEPS
1. Put a small amount of dry yeast on a slide. Examine it closely.
2. In a small bowl, mix cold water with yeast.
3. In a different bowl, mix warm water—but not steaming—with yeast. Add a pinch of sugar to the mixture.
4. Take out a slide and place a small drop of the cold-water mix on it. If available, place a cover slip over it.
5. Examine your slide under the microscope. Write your observations in your *Science Smart Journal.*

— *continued on next page* —

continued from previous page

6. Take out a second slide and place a small drop of the warm-water mix on it. If available, place a cover slip over it.
7. Examine your second slide under the microscope. Write your observations in your *Science Smart Journal*.
8. Wait 5 minutes. Then look in the microscope again and in your *Science Smart Journal* describe what you see on both slides.

"So you see, even something as simple as yeast is made of cells. Every organism, whether it's a **complex organism** like an animal or a **simple organism** like bacteria, is made up of cells. A complex organism can be made up of millions of different cells, and a simple organism can be made up of just a single cell."

"Wait one minute," Bridget said with her mouth full of pizza, "are you saying that I'm made of the same thing that yeast is."

"Not exactly," Barnaby said. "There are many different types of cells. Take a look," Barnaby said, pulling a cotton swab out of his pocket, swabbing the inside of his check, and then wiping it on microscope slide.

TRY IT YOURSELF!

Cells

MATERIALS
1 cotton swab, microscope, 3 microscope slides, 3 microscope slide covers, a very thin slice of cork, the mixture of warm-water, yeast, and sugar

STEPS
1. Swab the inside of your cheek with a cotton swab and then wipe your cotton swab on a slide.
2. Take out a second slide and place a small drop of the yeast mix on it.
3. Take out a third slide and put the thin slice of cork on it. (Ask an adult to create the thin cork slice for you.) You can also take a thin piece of onionskin from the surface of an onion.
4. Place each slide on the microscope and focus. In your *Science Smart Journal*, draw what you see on each slide.

"So why couldn't our ghost just have been like one gigantic cell?" Angie asked before Barnaby had even finished putting away the experiment.

"Tell me this: Does it take you less time to walk across the kitchen or across the country?" Barnaby asked, smiling.

"Duh," his sister said, "across the kitchen obviously."

"Think about it. A cell needs things like food and oxygen that are outside of it. And the essential parts of a cell are in the middle of the cell," Barnaby explained, reaching into his wild hair to grab yet another pencil. "Take a look at this."

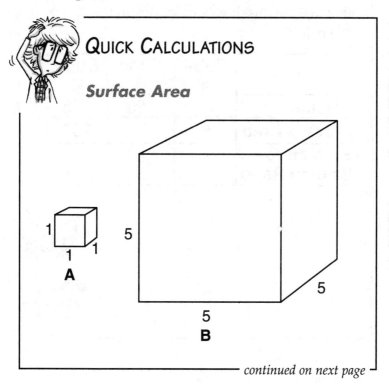

QUICK CALCULATIONS

Surface Area

continued on next page

continued from previous page

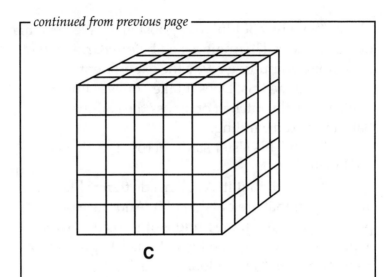

C

What are the missing calculations in the table below?

	Cube A	Cube B	Cube C
Volume		125	125
Surface Area	6		750
Surface-to-Volume Ratio	6	$\frac{5}{6}$	

"So you see," Barnaby explained, "the volume of cube B is $5 \times 5 \times 5$, or 125. Its surface area is $6 \times 5 \times 5$, or 150. Now even though cube C has the same volume as cube B, cube C has 125 individual cells, each with a surface area of 6. So its surface area is 6×125, or 750. That helps to explain why smaller cells are more helpful in an organism."

"Helpful to an organism," Bridget sniffed, "but it doesn't prove to me that there's no such thing as ghosts."

"So the smaller each cell is, the faster things can travel from one end of a cell to the other," Barnaby explained. "Our ghost would have some pretty big problems if he were just one huge cell. Having millions of cells also helps us grow."

"I grew four inches last year," Angie says, jumping down off her chair. "I'm the second tallest girl in my class. Jenny Ota is the tallest, but only by an inch."

"That's great, squirt," Bridget said, ruffling her hair. "You're just a crazy pile of cells."

"It's called **mitosis**," Barnaby interjected.

"My toes is what?" Babette asked, confused.

"In need of a coat of polish, I'll say that much," Bridget told her friend.

"I do not believe in using nail polish," Babette said defiantly. "I like the way my toes look *au naturale*."

"Mitosis," Barnaby explained, holding up his index finger, "one word."

"Right. Mitosis. One word. Sounds like fun," Bridget added, biting her finger to stifle her laughter.

"Well, if you like your cells splitting into two nuclei, then you're in luck," Barnaby told her.

"Okay, that sounds painful. What's a nuclei anyway? Isn't that what they make bombs out of?"

"You're thinking nuclear, not nuclei. 'Nuclei' is plural for **nucleus,** which is the part of the cell that controls all its activities and that contains all the information necessary for reproduction. The nucleus is the command center of a cell. Most cells, even if they're different in size, shape, or function, share some basic common features. Take a look at this," Barnaby added, pulling out a book out of his pocket.

ANIMAL CELL

Cell Membrane: covers the outside of the cell

Vacuoles: store water, food, and other materials

Cytoplasm: liquid center of the cell in which most of the cell's life processes occur

Chromosomes: contain instructions for cell development

Nucleus: controls the activities of the cell

Mitochondrion: transforms energy in food molecules into energy needed by cells

PLANT CELL

Cell Wall: rigid structure
that supports and protects the cell

Cell Membrane: covers the outside of the cell

Cytoplasm: liquid center of the cell in which
most of the cell's life processes occur

Vacuoles: store water,
food, and other materials

Chromosomes: have
chemical information
that instructs cell activity

Nucleus: controls the
activities of the cell

Mitochondrion: transforms energy in
food molecules into energy needed by cells

Chloroplasts: convert light energy into
chemical energy so that plants can make food

"Okay, fine," Bridget said, "there's no such thing as ghosts. I believe you now. But I don't get how these tiny cells know what they're supposed to do. It's not like I'm sitting here thinking, 'Vacuoles, store up some food. It's gonna be a long day.'"

"Well, a day is always the same length of time—twenty-four hours, I believe. But I see your point. Take a look at this," Barnaby said

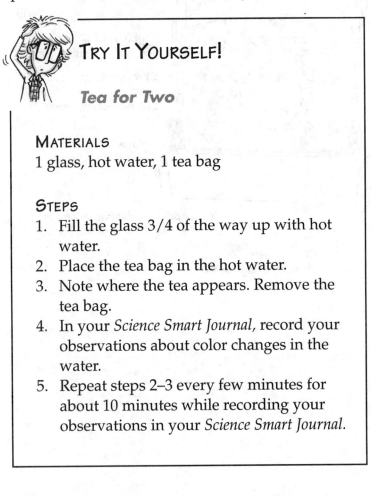

TRY IT YOURSELF!

Tea for Two

MATERIALS
1 glass, hot water, 1 tea bag

STEPS
1. Fill the glass 3/4 of the way up with hot water.
2. Place the tea bag in the hot water.
3. Note where the tea appears. Remove the tea bag.
4. In your *Science Smart Journal,* record your observations about color changes in the water.
5. Repeat steps 2–3 every few minutes for about 10 minutes while recording your observations in your *Science Smart Journal.*

"Now tell me this, Bridget: How does the tea bag know when to let water in and to let the tea out?" Barnaby asked.

"I don't know. It just kinda does, I guess," Bridget said cautiously.

"Precisely, uh, sort of," Barnaby said. "Imagine that the tea bag is like a cell and the tissue surrounding the tea is like a cell membrane. Cell membranes are **selectively permeable,** which means they allow some substances to enter the cell while keeping others out. The tea bag lets the water in and it lets the tea out. Like the tea bag, the cell membrane permits certain things to pass in and out of the cell. Except instead of letting in just water, the cell membrane lets all sorts of molecules into the cell."

"Wait, wait, wait," Angie cried, flailing her arms over her head. "Slow down. What are molecules?"

"Think of it this way, **molecules** are the smallest possible piece of a substance. For example, you've probably heard of H_2O. That's the chemical expression for a water molecule. If you just have one molecule of H_2O, you still have water. If you break it down any further, it's not water anymore. A glass of water has zillions and zillions of molecules of water, floating around, bumping into each other and rolling over each other. Each water molecule looks and acts exactly the same. Does that help?" Barnaby asked.

"I think I get it," Angie muttered quietly.

"Good, now to confuse matters even more. Molecules are in constant random motion. As they bump around, some of them bump into cell membranes and move in and out of cells. The molecules in motion inside the tea bag bump around and some hit the wall of the bag and bounce out. Now they're moving around in the water. That's the color you see coming out of the tea bag. It's an example of **diffusion,** which is the movement of molecules from an area of high concentration to one of low concentration."

"I get it!" Angie practically shouted. "There's a lot of tea in the bag but none in the water. The tea moves out of the bag and into the water. If we kept the bag in the water indefinitely, eventually it'd probably reach a point where there is a balance of tea in the bag and tea in the water. I'm right, right?"

"Precisely!"

"Are you telling me that molecules like to share?" Bridget asked unconvinced.

"I guess I am."

"So the cells in my body like to share," Bridget said.

"Well, diffusion of water through a cell membrane is called **osmosis.** It's essentially the same idea, though."

"Sharing?" Bridget asked curiously.

"Yes, I suppose so," Barnaby replied.

"Good," she said, taking a bottle of nail polish out of her pocket, "Babette, the cells in my body want to share this with you."

"You," Babette said, shaking her head, "are so American. I think Bridget's cells need brains."

"Well, cells don't really have brains, but they do help provide the brain with energy to function. Touch your forehead," Barnaby said then. "See how it's warm? What you're feeling is heat energy produced by **respiration,** which is a chemical process in which glucose molecules—like sugar—are broken down to release energy used by cells."

"How about we compromise?" Bridget said, ignoring Barnaby. "We'll paint Barnaby's toes."

"That idea," Babette said, "I like."

"The mitochondria," Barnaby said, backing into a corner, "plays a vital role in respiration, you know. Once the glucose is broken down, simple molecules enter the mitochondria, where they combine with oxygen to form water and carbon dioxide." He was practically yelling as the two girls wrestled his shoes off. Angie was giggling unstoppably at the sight, and Beauregard thought it best to make himself scarce. He scampered upstairs for a comfortable seat under a bed.

"Okay, okay, I give in," he said, "but let's try one quick experiment first."

TRY IT YOURSELF!

They're Good for Your Heart

MATERIALS
2 jars, cotton balls, 6 oz. dry beans, 6 oz. beans
that have soaked overnight, 2 thermometers

STEPS
1. Place the soaked beans in one jar and the
   dry beans in the other. Label both jars.
2. Fill both jars with cotton balls.
3. Insert a thermometer in each jar and take a
   reading of the temperature. Record the data
   in your *Science Smart Journal.*
4. Take the temperature of both jars every
   fifteen minutes for two to three hours.
   Record your data in your *Science Smart
   Journal.* Record why you think you got
   these readings. What theories can you
   draw from these outcomes?

"Forget the beans. Now, that's an experiment,"
Bridget said, standing proudly beside Babette,
examining their work on Barnaby. They'd fashioned a
striped look on his toenails—red, white, and blue—as
a sort of expression of American and French unity.

"This comes off, right?" he asked.

"Of course," Babette said, smiling. "But it is
such a good look you should maybe reconsider."

"See what we can accomplish when we work together," Bridget said, high-fiving her friend.

"You two are acting just like cells in tissues," Barnaby asserted. When his two friends looked at him curiously, he added, "Groups of cells that work together to perform a function are called **tissues.** For instance, the muscle cells in your heart work together to form heart tissue. Tissues that work together make up an **organ.** Your heart is a good example of an organ. In your heart muscle tissue and vein tissue, two of the many types of tissue, work together. And organs that work together to perform a life function form an **organ system.** Your digestive system and your respiratory system are two examples of organ systems. When organ systems work together, they act like paragraphs in a story to form a whole **organism**—such as you, me, Beauregard, and that plant on the windowsill."

"From top to bottom, it's all about sharing," Angie added.

"It sure is. It sure is," Barnaby said as he tried to get a good look at his toenails.

✎   ✎   ✎   ✎   ✎

Barnaby went upstairs to take the nail polish off with Angie's help. Bridget and Babette, stuffed with pizza and exhausted from the various experiments, slumped over to the couch to watch the game again. The Yankees had let in two runs in a long fifth inning and they were now trailing 5 to 3.

Bridget sighed, but she didn't seem too upset. "Your Yankees are losing, no?" Babette asked.

"Yeah, I suppose," she said.

"You should be more upset, I think," Babette suggested.

"I should be," said Bridget, smiling to herself. "It's just that Barnaby was so funny with his painted toenails and his crazy hair, still trying to explain the laws of science to us."

Babette nodded and giggled, "His hair is crazy, it is true. What family member did he get it from?"

Bridget furrowed her brow. She had met both of Barnaby's parents, and neither of them had the same kind of wild hair that Barnaby possessed. She looked at a family portrait on the wall and said, "I don't know. He seems to be the only one in the world with that kind of hair."

Hearing footsteps at the top of the stairs and curious about the mystery, Babette leaned toward her American friend and whispered in her ear, "Maybe you should ask him about it."

At that idea, Bridget got excited again. "Yes! Let's definitely ask Barnaby about it!"

"Ask Barnaby about what?" said Barnaby, as he hopped off the bottom step. He had cotton balls stuck between his toes and a bottle of nail polish remover in his pocket.

Laughing at the sight of Barnaby with cotton balls tucked between his toes, Bridget asked him, "Where did you get your crazy hair from?"

"My parents told me that it came from my great grandfather," replied Barnaby, ignoring the fact that the two girls were still laughing at him. "I never got to meet him, unfortunately. But he used to be a radio repairman, and apparently he kept an entire 20-piece set of tools in his hair. I can only fit about nine tools in my hair before they start to fall out."

Bridget fell off the couch laughing, and Babette walked up to Barnaby to get a closer look at his amazing hair.

"Tell me, Barnaby," said Bridget. "What do you know about heredity and reproduction?"

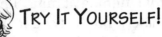

TRY IT YOURSELF!

Growing up, uP, UP

MATERIALS

4 young corn seedlings, permanent marker, centimeter ruler, 4 plastic bags, paper towels

STEPS

1. Label each plastic bag. Write "Corn Seedling A" on the first bag, "Corn Seedling B" on the second bag, "Corn Seedling C" on the third bag, and "Corn Seedling D" on the fourth bag.

2. Put one corn seedling in each of the plastic bags. Measure each seedling and write your measurements in your *Science Smart Journal*.

3. Moisten four sheets of paper towel. Carefully wrap each seedling in a piece of wet paper towel and place it back in the correct plastic bag.

4. After twenty-four hours measure each seedling again. Write your measurements in your *Science Smart Journal*.

— continued on next page —

continued from previous page

5. Repeat step 4 twenty-four hours later. Again, carefully record your measurements in your *Science Smart Journal*.

6. Figure out how much each root has grown. (Subtract the original length from the length 48 hours later.) Then calculate the average growth of all four roots.

7. Using what you've just learned about cell mitosis, write about what you've just observed. What do you think was necessary for this growth? Predict how much the roots might grow in 1 week, 1 month, and 1 year. If your seedling didn't grow, write why you think that happened.

✍ QUIZ #9 ✍
Matching

Match each word in the column below with its correct meaning on the next two pages.

1. Mitochondrion   _____

2. Tissues   _____

3. Cell wall   _____

4. Respiration   _____

5. Chloroplast   _____

6. Organ   _____

7. Nucleus   _____

8. Mitosis   _____

9. Osmosis   _____

10. Chromosome   _____

11. Organ system   _____

12. Molecule   _____

13. Diffusion   _____

14. Cell membrane   _____

15. Cytoplasm   _____

16. Permeability   _____

17. Cell   _____

18. Organism   _____

19. Vacuole   _____

A. A chemical process in which glucose molecules are broken down to release energy used by cells

B. Groups of cells working together to perform a function

C. The process in which cells split into two new cells, each with the same type and number of chromosomes

D. A part of an animal or plant in which tissues work together to do a particular job

E. Organs that work together to perform a life function

F. The part of the cell that converts light energy into chemical energy

G. The basic unit of all living things

H. The part of the cell in which water, food, and other materials are stored

I. A rigid structure that supports and protects plant cells

J. A semipermeable structure that covers the outside of the cell

K. The part of the cell that controls all its activities

L. The ability of a membrane to allow some substances to enter the cell while keeping others out

M. The smallest particle a compound can be broken into without changing its identity

N. The movement of molecules from an area of high concentration to one of low concentration

O. The part of a cell that transforms energy in food molecules into energy needed by cells

P. Diffusion of water through a cell membrane depending on the concentration of solutes on either side

Q. The highest level of cellular organization; something that is alive

R. The liquid part of the cell in which most of the cell's life processes occur

S. The structure of a cell that contains instructions that "tell" a cell how to develop

Chapter 6

Reproduction and Heredity

Barnaby sat on the couch next to his friends and rested his cotton-balled feet on the coffee table. "It's an extraordinarily interesting and complex topic. **Reproduction,** the process by which organisms produce young, and **heredity,** the passing of traits from one generation to the next, are essential characteristics of all living systems."

"Look," Bridget said, "the Yankees just let in another run. Wow, isn't baseball great? Why don't we all watch in silence? Just to get the full impact."

"That's so interesting," Babette said, casually picking up the remote control and turning off the television. "Tell us more."

"Actually," Barnaby said, clearing his throat, "it's not really my area of expertise."

"In France," Babette continued as Angie ran in and jumped up on her brother's lap, "it's one of the first things they taught me about in science class. They say there are two kinds of cells—body cells and sex cells."

Angie clapped her hands together. "Go on please, Professor."

"Well," Babette said, "it is all very simple. **Body cells,** such as blood cells and skin cells, copy themselves—reproduce, if you will—through mitosis. That's what we were talking about before."

Babette continued, "**Sex cells** are what some organisms use to produce offspring. Female sex cells are called **eggs.** Male sex cells are called **sperm.** Females have egg cells, and males have sperm cells."

"Follow me," Babette said, heading straight for the kitchen.

TRY IT YOURSELF!

Eggs!

MATERIALS
1 raw egg, 1 bowl

STEPS
1. Gently crack a chicken egg into a bowl.
2. Examine the shell. In your *Science Smart Journal*, consider how the shell might be helpful to a developing chick.
3. Draw a diagram of the egg in the bowl in your *Science Smart Journal*. Infer what you think might be the function of each part of the egg.

"Chickens have adapted their reproduction so that their species continues to live," Babette explained. "It's remarkable, no? What do you think, Barnaby?"

"Fascinating," he said, nodding his head. "But don't different species reproduce in different ways?"

"Absolutely," Babette said. "There's **sexual reproduction** and **asexual reproduction.** Sexual reproduction differs from asexual reproduction because it begins when sperm from a male unite with eggs from a female in a process called **fertilization.** And even in sexual reproduction, there's **external fertilation** and **internal fertilization.**"

"I think I hatched from an egg," Bridget joked.

"Well, if your parents practiced *external* fertilization, you probably did hatch. For many water-bound animals, egg and sperm cells unite outside the organism. The female releases her eggs into the water, and the male then releases his sperm, which swim to the eggs. Fish and frogs reproduce this way, for example. *Internal* fertilization means the female keeps the eggs inside her. The male deposits his sperm inside the female's body, and the sperm swim to unite with the eggs. Once fertilized, the eggs develop inside the female's body," Babette explained, clapping her hands together.

"Let's pretend that I was born by that mitosis process. That'd suit me just fine," Bridget explained to her friend.

"I doubt it. Mitosis, or asexual reproduction," Babette explained, "means no sperm, no eggs, and just one parent. Some plants reproduce asexually. For example, sponges—not the kind in the kitchen—can split in two and create a whole new sponge. That new sponge could be broken up into thousands of other sponges, and they'd all be identical to the original sponge. So unless you're a sponge in disguise, you are probably not a product of asexual reproduction."

"Well, maybe I am," Bridget responded.

"I do not think so," Babette said. "Offspring from asexual reproduction have exactly the same characteristics as their parent. I have seen your father. He has curly hair and one eyebrow."

"My father doesn't have a uni-brow," Bridget protested. "He just worries a lot so he furrows."

"You forgot about the **chromosomes**," Barnaby piped in.

"Ah, yes," Babette agreed.

"Chromosomes," Barnaby said, "contain the instructions that 'tell' a cell how to develop. All species have a certain number of chromosomes. Dogs have 78 chromosomes, for instance. People have 46."

"In mitosis," Babette said, moving everyone over to a table directly under the light, "each new cell has the same number of chromosomes as its parent cell. In a process called **meiosis,** on the other hand, sex cells are created with only *half* of an animal's chromosomes. It is sort of like this," she added pulling out a poster board from under the table.

TRY IT YOURSELF!

Meiosis

MATERIALS
6 white note cards (or pieces of paper), 6 blue note cards (or pieces of paper), scissors, 4 equal pieces of string each about 6 inches long

STEPS
1. Use your four pieces of string to create one large circle on a table or desk.

continued on next page

2. Cut out two circles, two triangles, and two squares from your white note cards.

3. Put the two circles, two squares, and two triangles in the circle created by your string. Stack the identical shapes on top of each other. The circle represents Body Cell A.

4. Cut out two circles, two triangles, and two squares from your blue note cards.

5. Now stack those blue circles, squares, and triangles next to their "sister" shapes—the shapes that are their twins—inside Body Cell A. Your cell should look like it has one of each color and two of each shape, with the duplicates underneath.

6. Use the four strings from Body Cell A to create two smaller circles with two strings each. The two new circles represent Body Cell B and Body Cell C.

7. Move one stack of circles, one stack of squares, and one stack of triangles into Body Cell B. Move the other stack of circles, the other stack of squares, and the other stack of triangles into Body Cell C. (The colors may be mixed up at this point.)

8. Use the two strings from Body Cell B to create two smaller circles with one string

continued on next page

continued from previous page

each. Use the two strings from Body Cell C to create two smaller circles with one string each. The four new circles represent four sex cells: Sex Cells 1, 2, 3, and 4.

9. Separate each shape again. Separate the shapes from Body Cell B by moving one of each shape into Sex Cell 1 and the rest into Sex Cell 2.

10. Repeat step 9 by moving one of each shape from Body Cell C into Sex Cell 3 and the rest into Sex Cell 4.

"You see," Babette explained as she sketched a quick diagram on a stray piece of paper, "that is meiosis."

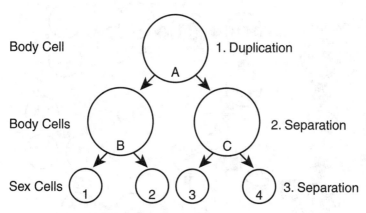

"It all begins in the reproductive organs," Babette continued. "It starts with just one cell, just like in Body Cell A, and it ends up with four cells that have only half the original number of chromosomes in them. The original chromosomes double, forming identical copies called **sister chromatids.** That happened in step 5, when we added the sister shapes. The doubled chromosomes then match up in pairs and separate, which we did when we split the shapes into Body Cells B and C. At that point, the first division of meiosis has occurred. The chromosomes then line up in the center of the cell again, then they move to opposite ends of the cell, and before you know it, the cells divide again just like when we broke them out into sex cells one, two, three, and four. Easy, peasy, lemon squeezy!"

"Here you go," Barnaby said, pulling down a dusty book off a nearby shelf and opening it to a dog-eared page. "This is what meiosis looks like."

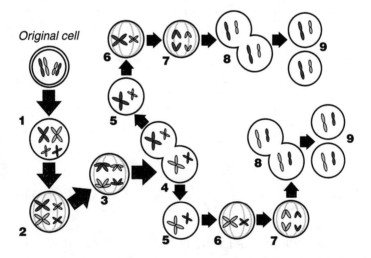

Angie still looked perplexed. "What I don't get," she said, "is why if Barnaby and I come from the same meiosis, the same chromosomes and all, why aren't we identical?"

Babette nodded. "To answer your question, Angie, let us do a quick experiment."

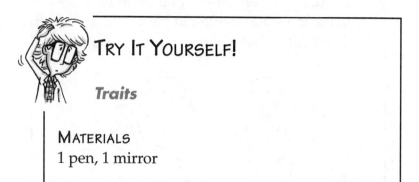

TRY IT YOURSELF!

Traits

MATERIALS
1 pen, 1 mirror

STEPS
1. In your *Science Smart Journal,* recreate the chart below.

Trait	Description of Yours
Eye Color	
Tongue Rolling	
Earlobe	
Hair Color	
Dimpled Chin	
Right- or Left-Handedness	

— *continued on next page* —

— *continued from previous page* —

2. Examine your ears in your mirror. Compare your earlobes to the pictures below. Are your earlobes attached or unattached? Record your observations in the table you created in your *Science Smart Journal.*

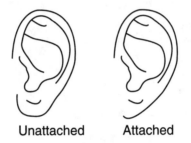

Unattached   Attached

3. Examine your tongue in your mirror. Try to roll your tongue into a 'U' shape. In the table in your *Science Smart Journal,* record whether you can roll your tongue or not.

4. Examine your chin in your mirror. In the table in your *Science Smart Journal,* record whether you have a dimpled chin or not.

5. Continue your examination until you have described all the traits listed on the chart.

"You see," Babette explained, "every living thing has certain unique characteristics. These are called **traits**. See how both Angie and Barnaby have attached earlobes and can roll their tongues? That is because traits are not random. People who are related have a far greater chance of sharing a certain trait. However, Barnaby has blond hair and Angie has brown hair. So just because you are in the same family doesn't mean you are identical."

"Duh," Angie said, "if I were identical to Barnaby, I'd be picking pencils out of my hair, too."

"To understand why you are not, we have to go all the way back to **Gregor Mendel,** an Austrian monk who did a series of experiments to show that traits in plants do not occur purely randomly," Babette explained. "Mendel studied pea plants. He noticed **variation,** the occurrence of different traits that make organisms different from each other within the same species. Of his pea plants, some had yellow seeds while others had green seeds. Some were short and others were tall. Particular variations kept occurring across generations, and he hypothesized that the parent plant controlled the variation."

"That still doesn't explain why Barnaby has that crazy hair and I don't," Angie said.

"I like Barnaby's hair," Bridget said.

"It does what it's supposed to do," Barnaby said, running his fingers through it and pulling out a handful of note cards. "Sort of."

"Your hair is different because of **dominant** and **recessive traits,**" Babette explained, shrugging.

"Dominant traits cover up or overpower most recessive traits, and recessive traits seem to disappear in the presence of dominant traits. For instance, when Mendel bred his pea pods, he found that when he crossed short plants with tall plants, the offspring were always tall. The short trait seemed to disappear, and so Mendel predicted that this was because tallness was the dominant trait."

"But then," Angie said slowly as if she were just figuring it out for herself, "why don't Barnaby and I have the same kind of hair? One trait should be dominant, right?"

"It would seem. But Mendel also noticed something strange. When he bred a short plant with a tall plant to get a tall plant, and then bred that new tall plant with a short plant, sometimes the offspring produced was short. 'How could that be?' he wondered."

"I'm wondering the same thing, frankly," Barnaby said, scratching his head.

"Barnaby," Bridget said, "you're confused."

"I wouldn't say confused," he stammered. "I'm just curious."

"Well, it is the difference between a **genotype** and a **phenotype**," Babette said. "A genotype is the genetic makeup of an organism. For instance, a plant with short and tall parents gets short and tall traits in its genes. Those are its genotypes. However, the phenotype is the way those traits are *expressed*. So because the tallness is the dominant trait, it overrules the short, recessive trait, and the plant's phenotype is tall. Let us play a little game. Maybe, Barnaby, it will help your curiosity."

TRY IT YOURSELF!

Making Mr. or Ms. Right

MATERIALS

1 pen, 28 colored note cards

STEPS

Dominant Trait	Recessive Trait
unattached earlobe (E)	attached earlobe (e)
brown hair (H)	red hair (h)
dimpled chin (C)	undimpled chin (c)
right-handedness (R)	left-handedness (r)
brown eyes (B)	green eyes (b)
rolling tongue (T)	non-rolling tongue (t)
widow's peak (W)	no widow's peak (w)

1. Divide the note cards in half. On the front of half the cards, write "male" and on the front of the other half write "female."
2. On the back of each card in the "male" pile, write a trait. Each of the fourteen dominant or recessive traits listed above should be listed on a note card.

— continued on next page —

— *continued from previous page* —

3. Repeat step 2 with the "female" pile.
4. Keeping the "male" and "female" cards separate, shuffle your cards.
5. Create a three-column table with seven rows in your *Science Smart Journal*. One column should say "genotype male," one "genotype female," and the other "phenotype."
6. Now you can start playing "Making Mr. or Ms. Right." Pick one card from the "female" pile and write the letter in the "genotype female" column in your table. For instance, if you pick "rolling tongue," write "T" in the space in the table. Then pick one card from "male" pile. For example, if you pick "green eyes," write "b" on the next line in the table in the "genotype male" column your Science Smart Journal.
7. Repeat step 6. You can only have one letter in a "genotype male" or "genotype female" table cell; when you pick a trait—such as attached or unattached earlobe—you should note the male and female genotype of the trait on the same line. (At some point, you will pick a card for a male or female genotype that you've already selected and added to chart. Simply discard that choice.)

— *continued on next page* —

continued from previous page

8. Once you have filled in all fourteen male and female genotypes, you're ready to see what Mr. or Ms. Right will look like. Write your male and female genotypes—let's say you have "C" and "C"—under the phenotype heading. Then check your chart for what the letters mean, and describe the trait. In this case—"CC"— Mr. or Ms. Right has a dimpled chin.

A completed chart might look like this:

Genotype Male	Genotype Female	Phenotype
B	B	BB—brown eyes
W	w	Ww—widow's peak
E	E	EE—unattached earlobe
h	h	hh—red hair
r	R	rR—right-handedness
T	T	TT—rolling tongue
C	C	CC—dimpled chin

Remember: Dominant traits always cover up the recessive trait. Mr. or Ms Right's phenotype will be the recessive trait if both your male and female genotypes are of that recessive trait.

"So you see," Babette explained, "it is simple. Because there are thousands of different traits and millions of different combinations of those traits, there is much variation in organisms that is produced as a result of meiosis."

"What I don't understand, though," Angie asked, raising her hand but not waiting to be called on, "is where this dominant and recessive information is stored."

"In your **genes,**" Babette answered. And, as if on cue, Angie pulled the front pockets of her jeans inside out and said, "Huh?"

"Not J-E-A-N-S," said Babette, spelling it out, "G-E-N-E-S! It is the place in a chromosome that controls a certain trait."

"Ugh," Bridget said, growling, "what's going on with my Yankees?" And with that, she turned to head upstairs.

"Bridget!" Babette yelled after her. "Do not run away to your bat and ball game."

"Hey guys," Bridget yelled back down, "Someone left the basement door open!"

"Uh oh," Angie moaned.

"Has anyone seen Beauregard?" Bridget thought to ask.

One after the other, they each said, "I haven't." Babette and Angie raced upstairs after Bridget. Barnaby opted to search the basement. They checked under every piece of furniture—under the chairs and tables, beds and bureau. They called his name. They opened a can of tuna as loudly as they could. They even made barking sounds to try to scare the poor cat out. Nothing worked.

But then, Barnaby yelled from downstairs, "Guys! Guys, come quick." The three girls sprinted— two steps at a time down the stairs—back down into the basement. Barnaby was hunched over the far corner.

The first thing out of Bridget's mouth was "Oh my god, is he okay?"

"I don't know," Barnaby said, turning away from the wall to reveal a strange crack barely large enough to crawl through, "but look at this."

Bridget moved forward and stuck her head in, unafraid of the consequences. When she turned back to her friends, her face told the whole story. Her eyes were opened wider than anyone had ever seen, and her mouth hung open, lips parted in the shape of a lazy "O."

"I know," Barnaby said, "it's like a whole different world in there."

"You don't think . . . " Bridget began.

"I don't know," Barnaby said, "but he's not down here, and he's not upstairs."

"You don't want to go in that crack in the wall, do you?" Angie said. "It can't be safe, Barnaby."

"We have no choice," Bridget said, her hands on her hips.

"We have no choice but to what?" Babette asked.

"To go in after him," Barnaby explained.

"We're really going in after him?" Angie said, swallowing hard.

"He's our friend," Bridget added, gathering her courage. "We have to."

"Let us go then," Babette said. "If it must be, it must." And one after the other, each wishing for luck, the children slipped through the hole in the wall and away into the other world below the basement.

TRY IT YOURSELF!

Punnett Squares

A Punnett square is a tool for showing possible combinations of gene pairs for any given trait. For instance, if you were crossing tall pea plants (TT) with short pea plants (tt), here's how you might construct your Punnett square.

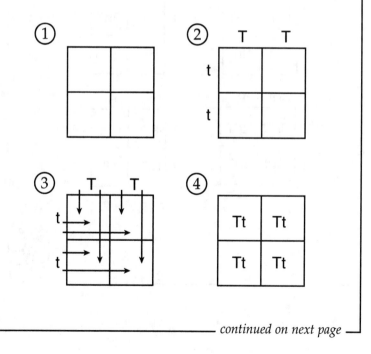

— *continued on next page* —

continued from previous page

1. In your *Science Smart Journal*, draw a Punnett square that shows the offspring of a woman with a dimpled chin (Dd) who married a man without a dimpled chin (dd), if a dimpled chin is the dominant trait. (There is more than one correct answer.)

2. With two traits, you will have four letters instead of two in your Punnett square. Which of the following is correct, if you cross one pea plant that has round seeds and is short (RRtt) with a pea plant that has wrinkled seeds and is tall (rrTt)?

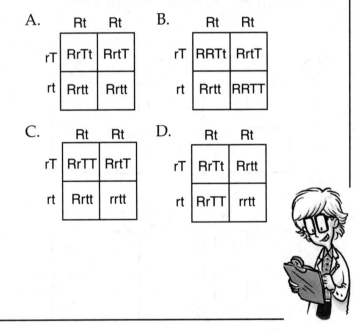

A.

	Rt	Rt
rT	RrTt	RrtT
rt	Rrtt	Rrtt

B.

	Rt	Rt
rT	RRTt	RrtT
rt	Rrtt	RRTT

C.

	Rt	Rt
rT	RrTT	RrtT
rt	Rrtt	rrtt

D.

	Rt	Rt
rT	RrTt	Rrtt
rt	RrTT	rrtt

✍ QUIZ #11 ✍
Matching

Match each word in the numbered column below with its correct meaning in the column on the next pages.

1. Traits _____

2. Phenotype _____

3. Eggs _____

4. Body cells _____

5. Recessive traits _____

6. Reproduction _____

7. Gregor Mendel _____

8. Meiosis _____

9. Internal fertilization _____

10. Chromosome _____

11. Dominant trait _____

12. Genotype _____

13. Sperm _____

14. Gene _____

15. Variation _____

16. External fertilization _____

17. Sex cells _____

18. Sister chromatids _____

19. Heredity _____

20. Sexual reproduction _____

A. A section of a chromosome that controls a trait in an organism
B. The reproduction process in which the female releases eggs into water, and the male's sperm swim to the eggs and fertilize them
C. Female sex cells
D. The specialized cells that some organisms use to produce offspring
E. The process by which sex cells are created
F. The result when original chromosomes double, forming identical copies of themselves
G. The process in which the sperm from a male organism unites with one or more eggs from a female
H. The passing of traits from one generation to the next
I. Process by which sperm unite with eggs inside the female body
J. The structure in a cell that contains instructions that "tell" a cell how to develop
K. A characteristic of a living thing that will always express itself if it is contained in an organisms genes

L. The occurrence of different traits that make organisms different from each other within the same species
M. The unique characteristics of a living thing that were inherited
N. The way genetic traits are expressed
O. Male sex cells
P. Cells that have been specialized to do certain jobs, such as blood and skin cells
Q. Characteristics of living things that are not expressed in the presence of dominant traits
R. The genetic makeup of an organism
S. An Austrian monk who did a series of experiments to show that traits do not occur purely randomly
T. A chemical process by which organisms produce young

Chapter 7

Ecosystems

"Barnaby, I don't think we're in Kansas anymore," Angie said, looking around at the lush, green foliage and the rainbow that roped in front of a gigantic waterfall. It might have been nighttime in the real world, but in this world—through the crack in the basement—the sun hung overhead as if it were high noon.

"We weren't in Kansas before anyway," Bridget said. Just then an eagle swooped down from the sky, pulled a field mouse out of the brush, and flew away.

"Wha . . . " Barnaby said, amazed.

"Beauregard!" Angie yelled as she was suddenly very worried about how a cat would survive in a place like this. The sky was thin-veined with wisps of clouds, and the grass was knee-high—perfect for losing someone of Beauregard's height.

Babette lifted her sunglasses and surveyed the scene. "C'mere, kitty, kitty, kitty," she called, and then turning to her friends, she said, "I don't know how we'll ever find him here."

"We can't just give up," Angie said, as tears welled up in her eyes.

"Of course not," Barnaby said, "we just have to be logical."

"Okay, Mr. Logical," Babette said, "what do we do now?"

"Easy," Bridget cut in. "Where do we always find Beauregard?"

"Lying in the sun," Angie shouted out.

"Precisely," Bridget said, mocking Barnaby, and then she nodded toward a plateau in the distance just over the tops of the trees. "If I know Beauregard, that's where we'll find him."

"But, but," Angie stammered, "how will we know how to get back?"

"Allow me," Barnaby said, pulling a pad and pencil out his hair. "Make fun of my hair, will you?" he added, winking at Angie. "This is an entirely unique **ecosystem.** That means there are organisms interacting with each other and with the nonliving environment. Everything works together as a single functional unit. So, I will take very detailed notes on our trip to find Beauregard."

"Good enough for me," Bridget said, clapping her hands together. "Let's go."

TRY IT YOURSELF!

Investigate Your Own Ecosystem

MATERIALS
1 pen

Imagine you were Barnaby. What would you find if you looked closely at the ecosystem of your own neighborhood?

STEPS
1. Choose a small area near your home to study the local plants and animals. Try to find out where and how those animals live, and how the nonliving parts around them influence how they live.
2. Write down any observations you make in your *Science Smart Journal.*

As the four friends tromped off in search of Beauregard, the terrain changed from a grassy plain to a forest. The sun poked through the treetops like the flickering light of a movie projector, casting odd speckled shadows on the ground. They could hear the rustling of small forest creatures all around. The occasional bird swooped across their path. They were mostly beautifully colored and long-beaked, with wings wider than their bodies. "Such a **habitat,**" Barnaby said, taking fast notes in his notebook, "a particular place where a wide variety of organisms live, I've never seen before."

"Look over there," Angie said, pointing to a small family of deer feasting on the leaves of a strange shrub.

"There used to be quite a big deer **population** living in our hometown," Barnaby said, "before all the buildings and roads destroyed the deer's habitat. It's ironic in a way. We build communities for our own comfort, but we often don't live well in a **community** in the scientific sense of the term. A community is a population of different animals living and interacting in a specific location."

Babette wasn't listening. She was too busy watching a striped animal gallop across the plains. "Is that—how do you say?—a zebra?" Babette asked.

"That is very odd," Barnaby said. "Deer, I can understand. Zebra, that's unheard of in North America. The tall, coarse grass probably makes the perfect meal for a zebra."

"At least they eat grass and not bugs," Bridget said, holding back a branch for her friends to pass by. "My brother used to have a lizard that we had to feed bugs. It was so gross."

"I've read that some people eat bugs," Barnaby said.

"Well, French people eat frogs. You can't get much nastier than that," Bridget said.

"Someday, when you grow up, you will understand," Babette told her friend.

"We're the same age!" Bridget quipped back.

"In Europe we mature much faster than you do in America," Babette explained. "I think watching so much television stunts your growth."

"See that?" Barnaby interrupted, pointing to a bird resting on the nearby branch. "It's a Cape May warbler, I believe. Fascinating. You see the Cape May has an important **niche**—or role—within the community. It feeds on the top outer branches of trees. Every species within a habitat has its own niche. That way they aren't competing for the exact same food sources. That's how so many populations are able to coexist."

"Did you hear that?" Bridget asked, cupping a hand to her ear.

"Hear what?" Barnaby wanted to know, but Bridget shushed him. The four children stood as quietly as they could, their eight ears perked. In the distance, there was a faint rumbling, almost like the sound of fleeing footsteps after the final school bell rings. Suddenly a rush of scared birds flew by overhead, darkening the sky; underfoot, woodchucks, beavers, and field mice all scrambled past the children. The noise was growing louder by the moment.

Angie figured it out first. "Stampede!" she yelled. "Run for it, guys!" After a moment's hesitation and a terrified look cast four ways around, the kids took off, sprinting as fast as they could. Behind them, they could make out hundreds of elephants. A stray elephant ran right between the kids without seeming to notice that it had nearly trampled four lost children.

"Over there," Barnaby yelled, pointing to a small, dark cave. "It's our only chance."

"Good call," Bridget said. But as she turned and headed for the cave, her foot got caught in a tangled tree root. She tripped, sprawling out in the dirt. No one noticed until after Barnaby had followed Angie and Babette safely inside the cave.

"Bridget, oh no!" Babette screamed, leaping to her feet, scrambling out after her friend. Angie leapt to her feet to follow and help, but like a good older brother, Barnaby held her back. The elephants seemed to be gaining speed. Bridget had almost managed to untangle her ankle as Babette approached and bent down next to her.

"I think I twisted it," Bridget said, on the verge of tears.

"Too bad," Babette said quickly. "No time for tears now." And with Bridget's arm over Babette's shoulder, the elephants only steps behind now, the girls did their version of the three-legged race, hobbling as quickly as they could toward the cave. They dove into the cave just as the elephants rumbled by, kicking up dust and trampling brush. The children watched in amazement. There were hundreds of gigantic elephants, all heading in the same direction. When they'd finally passed, the forest was quieter than ever.

"Are you okay?" Barnaby asked, gently touching Bridget's ankle.

"Yeah, yeah," she said pulling away, "I'll live."

"I know that," he said, "but can you walk?"

"I think so," she said, standing and then wincing in pain and sitting back down.

"We should go back," Babette said.

"I'm fine. I'm fine," she said, standing. "I'll just be a little slow."

"Here, you'll need your strength," Barnaby said, pulling a handful of fresh blackberries from a bramble just outside the cave. "This should help."

"Okay," she said, taking a cautious step and then popping a berry into her mouth. "I guess I'm finding my niche in this ecosystem."

"True, true," Barnaby said. "It's funny: Everything in an ecosystem has a role. Organisms can be classified as **producers, consumers,** or **decomposers.** Animals, such as zebras or elephants, that eat other animals or plants are called consumers. Plants that make their own food from sunlight, such as trees and grass, are called producers."

"So then what does that make me?" Bridget asked.

"Technically, you're a consumer," Barnaby said, considering Bridget seriously for a moment. "But maybe you should have your own category."

"So then what's a decomposer?" Angie asked.

"See this log?" Barnaby said, standing to turn over the log he'd been sitting on. "See the mold on it? That's a decomposer. It gets its food by breaking down dead organisms into nutrients. The mold is like a mushroom, for instance."

"Or a zombie," Bridget cut in.

"Not quite," Barnaby said slowly.

"So then Mozart would be a decomposing composer, right?" Angie asked laughing at herself.

"Very good," Barnaby said, making his sister smile. "The truth is that producers, consumers, and decomposers help energy pass through the ecosystem. Plants can produce their own energy from sunlight. That's why they're called *producers*. Remember those chloroplasts back in plant cells?

They are the plant-food factories that turn sunlight into sugar energy. When animals eat (consume) plants, they get some of that energy. That's why they're called *consumers.* When plants and animals die, decomposers get energy out of them and return their nutrients back to the soil. Each organism in this relationship is like a link in a chain. In fact, the **food chain** is a model that demonstrates how energy is passed from organism to organism in an ecosystem. However, because most organisms get their food from more than one source, food chains link to form what's called a **food web.** Take a look at this," Barnaby added, beginning a sketch in the dirt with a stick.

TRY IT YOURSELF!

Connect the Web

MATERIALS
1 pen

STEPS
1. Think about what each organism pictured on the next page eats. Draw arrows connecting each organism to its food. Make each arrow point from the food toward the organism that is doing the eating. Remember, each organism probably eats more than one thing.

continued on next page

2. Looking at your food web, think about whether, for instance, the mushroom is any more or less important in your web than the deer. Write your thoughts down in your *Science Smart Journal.*

"So, in a way," Barnaby said, "we're all connected. It's like a conspiracy of life. Without the flowers and the bugs, it would be pretty tough to survive."

"Well, I think we might have a tough time anyway," Babette said after she'd stuck her head outside the cave to make sure that the coast was clear. It was frighteningly quiet, though the forest looked like someone had plowed a road down the middle of it. Gray clouds were gathering, and off in the distance, a bolt of lightning crackled. "It is going to rain soon," Babette told her friends. "I think we have to head back to the basement."

"But Beauregard," Angie complained. "We can't just leave him."

"Beauregard is a very resourceful little cat. He will have to care for himself, I think," Babette said.

"And if we get caught out here, who knows how long we'll be lost. And frankly," Bridget said, "your parents might already be home by now. If they are, they're probably worried out of their minds."

"Bridget is right, Angie," Babette sighed. "We have no choice."

But Angie crossed her arms and said, "I'm not leaving without Beauregard," while at the same instant another crack of lightning sounded.

"Sorry," Barnaby said, hefting Angie up over his shoulder.

"Put me down!" Angie screamed as the friends plunged back down the path that the elephants had trampled for them. "I'm not leaving Beauregard. I don't care about the rain."

"Now, now," Barnaby told his sister as they began to walk back home. "Don't get hysterical. The rain is part of the natural cycle of life. Organisms need rain, sunlight, and nutrients to survive."

"I don't care, Barnaby," Angie cried as she beat her fists against Barnaby's back. Barnaby continued regardless. He couldn't think of any other way to calm his sister.

"Nearly all the energy that fuels life comes from sunlight," he began.

"Put me down!" Angie hollered.

"Plants, as I said, change sunlight into energy through a process called **photosynthesis.** Plants have molecules called **pigments** in their cells that absorb light energy. See?" Barnaby said, grabbing a leaf down off a tree.

TRY IT YOURSELF!

It's Not Easy Being Green

MATERIALS
2 sheets of newspaper, 1 handful fresh leaves, 1 piece of notebook paper, 1 small mallet

STEPS
1. Lay the sheets of newspaper on the table to protect the table. Stack four or five leaves on the paper.

— continued on next page —

┌─ *continued from previous page* ─────────────

2. Cover the leaves with the notebook paper.
3. Pound on the paper with the small mallet until a colored area appears.
4. Repeat step 3 after the notebook paper dries.
5. Write your observations in your *Science Smart Journal*.

"The leaves are green due to **chlorophyll,** which is the main pigment involved in photosynthesis. Can you tell me the difference between sunlight and other things plants need, such as water and nutrients?" Barnaby asked.

"I don't care," Angie said, trying desperately to seem uninterested.

Barnaby adjusted his grip on his sister and continued explaining himself. "Sunlight is virtually inexhaustible, meaning it can never run out (at least not for millions and millions of years). Water and nutrients are constantly being used and recycled. Take, for example, the **water cycle.** Energy from the sun causes water to evaporate. The water rises into the atmosphere. As the evaporated water rises, it cools and the water condenses into droplets in clouds. And then eventually the water falls down from the clouds as rain and returns to the ground. Pretty cool, eh? Plants get water from the soil and animals get water, amongst other means, by eating plants. We're all connected," Barnaby continued, locking his fingers together to illustrate.

"So what about the nutrients, then?" Angie asked, through gritted teeth, as if she didn't really want to ask but couldn't help herself.

"Good question. Take the **nitrogen cycle,** for example. We all need nitrogen to build proteins. There's nitrogen in the air, but that's useless to most species. Fortunately, plankton and bacteria convert the gas into a form that plants can use. When an animal eats a shrub, it gets nitrogen. And then if another animal eats that animal—bingo!—more nitrogen. See," Barnaby said, pulling a note pad and pencil from his lab coat, "check this out."

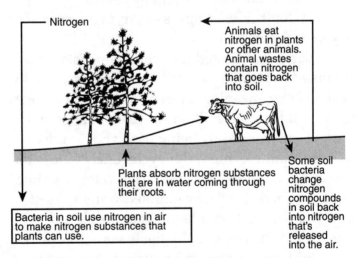

"There is one last thing all animals need to survive, right?" Barnaby asked.

"Well, duh," Angie said as Barnaby let her down, "oxygen."

"You're going to behave now, right?" Barnaby asked.

"Yes," Angie sighed, and then her thoughts turned to Beauregard, "but you promise we'll come back tomorrow and find Beauregard?"

"Of course, we will," Babette said, "but listen to your brother first, he wants to describe the **oxygen–carbon dioxide cycle.**"

"Well, we do need oxygen if we want to breathe. Think about it: If we're all breathing oxygen, shouldn't it all get used up? The cool thing is that during photosynthesis plants take in carbon dioxide and release oxygen. The oxygen you are breathing in right now probably came out of some plant not so long ago! So you see, we all depend on each other."

"Look," Bridget yelled, pointing toward a glowing crack in the ecosystem. "There's the opening!" One after another, the children slipped back into the basement.

"It must be midnight by now," Barnaby said dusting himself off. "Mom and Dad are going to kill me."

"But," Babette said, pointing at the clock, "why does the clock say it's only five minutes later than when we left?"

"I didn't miss the game?" Bridget yelled, jumping up and down clapping. She sprinted up the stairs and threw open the door, and as if nothing had happened, Beauregard slipped right past her and meowed.

"Beauregard!" Angie squealed, scooping the cat into her arms and peppering him with kisses. "You're okay!" Beauregard pulled his head away and gave Angie a look as if to say, "Why shouldn't I be?"

"But, then what was. . ." Barnaby said, turning around to look at the opening in the wall. "It's gone!"

The kids stared at each other in disbelief. Their porthole had disappeared. Barnaby rubbed his eyes and shook his head, astonished. He ran a hand through his hair to give himself a moment to think, and he felt something that must have somehow become stuck in his mane of knots. It took him a careful moment, and a little painful pulling, before he freed a strange spotted egg from his hair. "Guys," he said, holding it an arm's length out, "what's this?"

"I don't know," Bridget said as if he were accusing her of something. "It's not some kind of weirdo French haute cuisine, is it?"

"No," Babette said evenly, "it is not."

"Well, whatever it is," Angie said, noting the shaking on the outside of the shell, "it looks like it's about to hatch."

Angie, Babette, and Bridget stared in amazement. The egg rattled, quivered, and cracked. The girls' eyes grew wide. They couldn't believe what they saw sitting in the palm of Barnaby's hand.

✍ **QUIZ #12** ✎

TRY IT YOURSELF!

In the Desert

Every ecosystem puts different demands on the animals and plants that live in it. For instance, water is scarce in the desert. Conserving water is an important task for anything that lives in the desert. Do the following experiment to see how you can help your "animal," represented by a sponge, adapt to the harsh desert conditions.

MATERIALS
1 soaking wet sponge, water, scale

STEPS
1. In your *Science Smart Journal* brainstorm ways to help your wet sponge conserve water over a twenty-four-hour period. You can do anything you want to keep your sponge from drying out, except add more water. You must leave it in the open for at least four hours during the twenty-four-hour day. Remember, animals in the desert can't hide from the sun all day. They have to go out to scour for food, too. Write down how you plan to keep your sponge wet and your predictions of results in your *Science Smart Journal.*

—— *continued on next page* ——

continued from previous page

2. In your *Science Smart Journal,* design a table to record times and weights throughout the experiment.

3. Place your dripping wet sponge on a scale. Carefully record the time and weight in your *Science Smart Journal.*

4. Right after you've completed step 3, protect your sponge according to your plan. Take your sponge out whenever you want, but make sure that it is in the open for at least four hours.

5. At the end of the twenty-four-hour period, weigh your sponge again and record the time and weight in your *Science Smart Journal.*

6. Think about how effective your plan was. Describe why you think it was successful or not in your *Science Smart Journal.*

✍ QUIZ #13 ✎
Matching

Match each word in the column below with its correct meaning in the column on the next page.

1. Population _____

2. Consumer _____

3. Ecosystem _____

4. Community _____

5. Food web _____

6. Producer _____

7. Habitat _____

8. Photosynthesis _____

9. Food chain _____

10. Niche _____

11. Decomposer _____

12. Chlorophyll _____

13. Pigments _____

A. A model that demonstrates how energy is passed from organism to organism in an ecosystem
B. The main pigment that is involved in photosynthesis
C. A particular species that lives in a particular place during a particular time
D. An organism that makes its own food
E. Anything that breaks down dead organisms, returning their energy to the soil
F. A population of different animals living and interacting in a specific location
G. An animal's role in its environment
H. A community of organisms interacting with each other and with the nonliving environment
I.   An animal that eats other animals or plants
J.   The process by which plants change sunlight into energy
K. A combination of food chains in an ecological community
L. Molecules that absorb light energy
M. A particular place in which an organism lives

Chapter 8
Adaptation, Evolution, and Diversity

The egg shuddered first before a crack splintered down its side. The children stood still, fascinated, eyes fixed on the lizardlike head that poked out. With a push and a cry, the shell broke away; in Barnaby's hand, as amazing as it was, was a baby dinosaur. It smiled widely, showing off the littlest dinosaur teeth, and it was dressed in the softest lizard scales.

Barnaby raised it to eye level to get a closer look. The creature let out another plaintive, soft cry, and it dug its talons gently into Barnaby's soft palm, just enough to hurt a bit. Barnaby yelped and without thinking dropped the poor, frightened thing. If it hadn't started flapping its wings, it would have hit the floor with a thud. But thankfully it figured quickly, if a bit wobbly, that it could fly, and it zipped around the room before landing on Barnaby's shoulder.

"Uh, guys," Barnaby said, "I think we brought back a baby dinosaur."

"It's so cute," Bridget cooed, stepping closer to take a look. She held out a finger and the baby dinosaur licked her gently.

"It's not cute. It's supposed to be **extinct**. That means it doesn't exist anymore. The whole species of dinosaurs died out eons ago," Barnaby said.

"It thinks you're its Momma," Angie said.

"That is so sweet," Bridget said, hands clutched to her heart.

"We need to give it a name, no?" Babette said. "Let's call him Jean-Claude!"

"We are *not* calling our dinosaur Jean-Claude," Bridget told her friend. "It needs to be called something cool like Rocky or Spike."

"Spike?" Babette dismissed with a wave of her wrist. "How American."

"Spike is a great name. My uncle's name is Spike," Bridget shot back.

At that point, Angie cut in. "He's going to have enough trouble fitting in. Let's give him a more common name. We should call him Bob."

The four kids looked at one another and nodded. There was no arguing with Angie's logic. Besides, "Bob" had a certain ring to it. Even Bob seemed to accept his new name. He sneezed on Barnaby's neck.

"At least that's decided," Barnaby said, wiping himself clean of dinosaur mucus. "It still doesn't make any sense, though, that we should have found a dinosaur. At the end of the Mesozoic era, about 65 million years ago, they all," he said, his voice turning to a whisper then, "died out." Bob's attention piqued, and he turned to Barnaby and made a noise that almost sounded like "huh?"

"Extinction, frankly, happens when an environment changes too quickly for a species to adapt. In the case of the dinosaurs, scientists theorize that a large meteorite hit Earth, kicking up giant dust clouds and starting global fires. Plants died from fire and a lack of sunshine; as a result, no one had anything to eat. We really only know about dinosaurs from their fossils. I know," Barnaby added, turning to Bob and pushing out his bottom lip, "pretty sad."

"Well, clearly they're not completely extinct," Bridget said, gesturing to Bob. "Do you think they like baseball?"

"How can you still be thinking about baseball now?" Babette asked. "We might have just discovered the last living dinosaur."

"So? He'll still be the last living dinosaur *after* the Yankees game."

"Take a look at this," Barnaby said, setting Bob down on an empty table.

 # TRY IT YOURSELF!

Fossils

MATERIALS
aluminum foil, modeling clay, plaster of paris, petroleum jelly, a stick, a shell

STEPS
1. Smooth the modeling clay onto a sheet of aluminum foil.
2. Firmly press the stick into the clay, and then remove it as carefully as possible so that an impression remains.
3. Carefully curl up the edges of the foil and clay to form a shallow bowl. Pour some plaster of paris over the impression of the stick and let it dry overnight.

continued on next page

continued from previous page

4. Make a second "bowl" out of modeling clay. Cover the outside with aluminum foil. Rub petroleum jelly onto the shell and press it into the bottom of your "bowl."
5. Pour some plaster of paris over the shell so that it is completely covered and allow it to dry overnight.
6. The next day carefully remove the foil, clay, and shell from the hardened plaster "bowls."
7. In your *Science Smart Journal* describe what you've made.

Bob made a strange, happy gurgling sound, and then flicked his tongue across Angie's face like she was an ice cream cone. From out of nowhere, Beauregard hopped up on the table then and hissed at Bob. Angie was about to step in between them, but Beauregard lunged before she could. Fortunately, Bob was quicker than both of them, and he flapped his wings and flew to a perch on top of the bookcase. "Beauregard," Angie yelled, "stop that!" She scooped the cat up, carried him upstairs, and tossed him gently into her bedroom. "It's not very nice to attack extinct creatures," she warned, waggling a finger in the cat's direction.

Beauregard, never satisfied without the last word, meowed right back at her.

"What I don't understand," Angie said, closing the door tightly before tramping down the stairs, "is why Bob couldn't adapt. Couldn't he have hid in a cave and just, like, ordered pizza for a while?"

"**Adaptation** doesn't happen overnight," Barnaby said. "It's a gradual process. And animals can't do it just because they want to or need to. Some animals are just born with an adaptation. An adaptation is a characteristic that helps an organism, such as a dinosaur, survive and reproduce in its environment. It's not just ducking into a cave. This new characteristic might involve physical, structural changes or changes in behaviors such as hunting for food."

"Do you mean that if the world was suddenly flooded with water, some of us would develop fins and some wouldn't?" Angie asked.

"In a way," Barnaby answered slowly, "but not really. It's not like we could suddenly sprout fins if a pipe burst and the basement started filling with water. Every species has **variations.** Variations are behaviors or traits that distinguish one organism from another of the same species. If there was a big flood, the animals that had a specific variation of their feet that made them more finlike might be able to survive better. Their finlike feet are the beginnings of an adaptation. Adaptations can take millions of years."

"The variations are because of recessive and dominant traits," Babette broke in. "Just like we talked about."

"Precisely! And sometimes the appearance of certain traits helps a species survive. Try this," Barnaby said, pulling a handful of marshmallows out of his pants pocket.

TRY IT YOURSELF!

Natural Selection

MATERIALS
1 piece of blue paper, 1 piece of white paper, 20 marshmallows, a watch with a second hand

STEPS
1. Get a partner. Put one piece of blue paper and one piece of white paper next to each other.
2. Have your partner turn her back to you. Scatter the 20 marshmallows around the white paper.
3. Ask your partner to turn around and give her 10 seconds to pick up, one at a time, as many marshmallows as possible. In your *Science Smart Journal*, note how many marshmallows your partner picked up.
4. Repeat steps 2 and 3, but scatter the marshmallows on the blue paper this time.
5. Record the results in your *Science Smart Journal* and record why you think you got these results.

"So you see," Barnaby explained, "it's easier to find the marshmallows on the blue paper than on the white paper."

"Mgphh hmphh," Bridget said, her mouth stuffed full of marshmallows.

"I have no idea how long those have been in my pocket, you know," Barnaby told Bridget. Bridget's eyes opened wide, and she spat the marshmallows out into the wastebasket.

"*So* ladylike," Babette said. Bridget, in response, simply curtsied.

"Think about the strawberry dart-poison frog. Unlike most frogs, the strawberry dart-poison is colored bright red," Barnaby said. "Why do you think that is?"

"Because," Angie said, throwing a hand up, "it's poisonous, right? It doesn't do its predators any good if they only know that after they've eaten him. So it's bright red as a warning of sorts—to protect it from predators."

"So then why is Bob green?" Barnaby countered.

"Exactly the opposite reason," Babette responded. "To help him hide."

"Precisely!" Barnaby exclaimed, waking Bob briefly enough for him to raise his head and then lie back down. "He's getting bigger, isn't he?" Barnaby asked. Bridget and Babette both nodded in unison. "Anyway, the whole point is that the animals best suited to survive *do* survive. And because they survived—for instance, the frog with the bright red skin—they are more likely to pass on the trait that helped them survive. It's called **natural selection.** Living things that are better adapted to their environments are more likely to survive and reproduce."

"Sometimes an organism has traits that it doesn't need anymore," Barnaby continued. "Let's take a trip back about, oh, 55 million years and think about the predecessor of the whale. Below their spines, whales have what is known as **vestigial structure,** which is a bodily structure that once was useful to an organism but no longer serves any purpose. It's a small t-shaped bone. Some scientists think this is evidence that whales evolved from doglike creatures; over the past few decades, fossil evidence has been discovered to support this theory. Plus, during early development, whale embryos have four limbs. The rear limbs disappear before birth and the front limbs turn into flippers. But remember this adaptation took more than 50 million years to develop. Adaptations occur very slowly."

Buried inside the back part of the whale's body is the vestigial hind-limb bone.

"Not always," Babette told Barnaby. "You've heard about the speckled pepper moth, I presume."

"The speckled pepper moth . . . Well, uh," Barnaby stammered, reddening a bit in his cheeks.

"In the early 1800s the speckled pepper moth was very common in much of England," Babette explained. "The black moth was extremely rare. But by the early 1900s the black moths were all around town, and the speckled pepper moth was as rare as, well, a dinosaur in the basement."

"I think you're right—he is getting bigger," Bridget said, looking up at Bob. "The bookcase is starting to sag a bit underneath him."

"Very interesting, Babette," Barnaby said, ignoring Bridget altogether. "But that could be as much a case of improved research methods as it could be an actual adaptation."

"Um, I think you are wrong," Babette told her friend. "Speckled pepper moths used to blend perfectly with lichens that grew on tree trunks. Predators couldn't easily see them. The black moths were more visible, meaning they were more easily spotted and eaten by predators. But in the late 1800s

England became highly industrialized; as the factories pumped smoke into the air, the lichens died and the trees turned black. In just a few years, the speckled pepper moths became more visible to predators and the black moths less visible. With each generation there were fewer speckled pepper moths.

"In the mid-1950s England passed clean-air laws, and ever since, the speckled pepper moths have started making a comeback. Sometimes natural selection is less gradual than at other times."

"Very interesting," Barnaby said, shaking his head. "It all goes back to good ol' **Charles Darwin.** He developed the theory of natural selection in the early 1800s after studying animals on the Galápagos Islands. He had four main points," Barnaby said, pulling a copy of Darwin's *On the Origin of Species by Means of Natural Selection* from the bookshelf below a rapidly growing Bob.

- "Number one," Barnaby said, clearing his throat, "organisms produce more offspring than can survive. For instance, a dandelion produces thousands of seeds in the hope that only a few will grow into another dandelion.
- "Number two: Variations exist within populations. Just like Angie has brown hair and I have blond hair.
- "Number three: Some variations are more advantageous for survival than others. When dandelion spores spread out, they all compete for water, light, and soil nutrients. The ones best suited to grow are the ones most likely to grow.

- "And number four: Over time those individuals with advantageous variations will survive and reproduce. Which brings us right back to Babette's moth example. Depending on the environmental conditions, either the black or the spotted pepper moth was better prepared to survive."

"Darwin figured all that out?" Angie said, eyebrow cocked.

"He had some help, of course. Before him, geologists had figured out Earth was much older than anyone had expected," Barnaby said. "But, yeah, he did it without copying anyone. Here, try this experiment just to give you an example of advantageous variations."

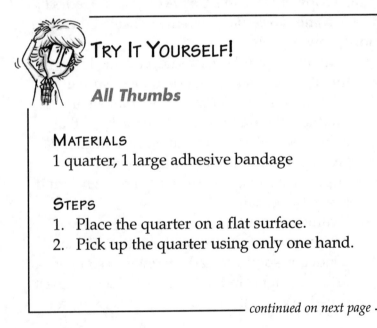

Try It Yourself!

All Thumbs

MATERIALS
1 quarter, 1 large adhesive bandage

STEPS
1. Place the quarter on a flat surface.
2. Pick up the quarter using only one hand.

continued on next page

— continued from previous page —

3. Bandage your thumb to your hand so that you can't move it. (Be careful not to do it so tightly that it hurts.)
4. Repeat steps 1 and 2 with your bandaged hand.
5. In your *Science Smart Journal,* note which was easier. Explain why and write down other things that opposable thumbs enable us to do. Opposable means the thumb can be positioned against the other fingers.

"So you see," Barnaby told everyone, "even humans have adapted to their environments. Our ancestors with opposable thumbs were best suited to survive and reproduce. Eventually, over millions of years, opposable thumbs became a dominant characteristic of our species. The humans with smaller, less opposable thumbs died off because they weren't able to get food as easily."

Just then, Bob awoke with a start. The bookshelf creaked, but, thankfully, it didn't collapse. Bob slipped down onto the ground, and only then did the children realize how large he'd become. In the space of just a half hour, he'd grown from being small enough to fit in Barnaby's palm to hovering over Angie, the second tallest girl in her class. Bob scratched himself with his wing and burped, politely covering his mouth. Without a word to any of the children, he made his way to the kitchen. The children then heard the refrigerator door open and shut, followed shortly after by the microwave opening, closing, and starting. The kids waited, huddled together, downstairs, unsure of what kind of creature they'd just unleashed on the world. The microwave bell went off, and then they heard the faint sounds of the ballgame coming from the television. Bridget strained to hear that the Yankees had fallen behind by another run. When the announcer said that Jason Giambi struck out, Bob grumbled angrily.

The four kids exchanged glances and then raced upstairs. "Bob?" Bridget said slowly. She was the first on the scene. "You like baseball?"

"That's what this is?" he said in a rather refined British accent. "I was hoping for something a bit more erudite," he added, holding out his wing as if to demonstrate his next point, "but I can't seem to change the bloody channel."

"See, natural selection," Bridget said, turning to Barnaby, "I bet that's why the dinosaurs went extinct."

"Because they couldn't switch stations on the television?" Barnaby said. "Doubtful."

"Not to be rude," Bob said, "but what's this about dinosaurs being extinct?"

"Well," Barnaby said slowly, "I don't know quite how to break this to you . . . "

"Do you want another frozen burrito?" Angie asked.

"They're really quite dreadful, you know," Bob said, nodding to the half-eaten one he'd left on the plate.

"Barnaby likes them," she explained.

"It's all I know how to cook," Barnaby confessed. "And I like cheese."

"I appreciate your candor. Now, if you don't mind, what's this about extinction?"

"You're sitting down?" Barnaby asked.

"So it appears," Bob replied dryly, and Barnaby, as best he could, started at the beginning.

✍ QUIZ #14 ✍

Natural Selection

As you've learned, species evolve through a process called natural selection. Organisms with favorable traits survive to reproduce. Look closely at the animals listed here. In your *Science Smart Journal,* list any outstanding traits you notice and think critically about why those traits may be favorable for that animal.

The cactus finch is a member of the seed-eating family of finches and is native to the tropical Galápagos Islands.

Cactus Finch

continued on next page

The snowshoe hare is native to North America. Its most distinguishing feature is its ability to camouflage itself. Its coat turns from reddish-brown in the summertime to white in the winter.

Snowshoe Hare

The desert cactus is a member of the cactus family, a group of spiny, fleshy plants native to arid sections of the Americas.

Desert Cactus

Orangutans are known as the great ape of Southeast Asia. They are most commonly found in trees in the jungles of Borneo and in northern Sumatra.

Orangutan

✍ QUIZ #15 ✍
Matching

Match each word in the left column with its correct meaning in the right column.

_____ 1. Extinct

_____ 2. Vestigial structure

_____ 3. Variations

_____ 4. Adaptation

_____ 5. Natural selection

_____ 6. Charles Darwin

A. A natural process through which organisms better adapted to their environment are more likely to survive and reproduce

B. The author of *On the Origin of Species by Means of Natural Selection*

C. Behaviors or traits that distinguish one organism from another of the same species

D. A characteristic that helps an organism survive and reproduce in its environment

E. A bodily structure that once was useful to an organism but no longer serves any purpose

F. When an organism doesn't exist anymore

Matching: Review

Match each word in the left column with its correct meaning in the right column.

___ 1. Osmosis

___ 2. Convection

___ 3. Photosynthesis

___ 4. Gregor Mendel

___ 5. Unbalanced forces

___ 6. Solubility

A. An Austrian monk who did a series of experiments to show that traits in plants do not occur purely randomly

B. Forces acting on an object unequally in some directions

C. A heat transfer by the motion of a heat-carrying medium

D. The process by which plants change sunlight into energy

E. The amount of a substance that can dissolve in 100 g of solvent at a given temperature

F. A diffusion of water through a cell membrane depending on the concentration of solutes on either side

Chapter 9
The Geosphere

"I'm afraid I don't understand," Bob said, crossing his wings. Barnaby had just spent half an hour explaining evolution and extinction, and Bob was determined not to believe that *all* the other dinosaurs were really gone. Frankly, he was having a bit of a panic attack. "But I can't be the last one," he said, breathlessly, as if there were something impossible in the suggestion. Which there was, because there shouldn't be any more dinosaurs anywhere, much less one in the living room watching Yankees playoff baseball and eating burritos.

"I know it doesn't make any sense," Barnaby kept repeating. "But Earth is a living planet, and it's constantly changing."

"This," Bob said in his proper British accent, stamping down his webbed foot, "is rock solid, unchanging, and eternal. How could this," he added, stamping his foot down again, "ever change enough that it couldn't support an entire species any longer?"

"Well, to explain that, we need to take a few steps back. First, we should talk about Earth's **geosphere,** which is the solid part of Earth. Look at this," Barnaby began, clearing a space on the coffee table.

TRY IT YOURSELF!

The Geosphere

MATERIALS
1 drawing compass, 1 centimeter ruler,
1 pencil, 1 square piece of cardboard,
3 markers—1 yellow, 1 red, 1 blue

STEPS
1. In the center of your cardboard, using the pencil, draw a circle with a diameter of 6.8 cm using your ruler and compass.

— continued on next page —

continued from previous page

2. Around the first circle, draw a second circle with a diameter of 12.6 cm using your ruler and compass.

3. Color the outer ring red and the inner circle yellow. Use your blue marker to draw a thin line around the outer edge.

"This is very crude drawing of the structure of Earth. The blue, thin outer edge represents the **crust**, which is made out of rock. Beneath the crust is a hot, solid layer called the **mantle**. And of course, at the center of Earth is a dense **core**. The core is actually split into a solid inner core and an outer core, which is hot and liquid."

"That's wonderfully interesting," Bob said dryly, "but that doesn't really help me, does it?"

"This is important background information," Barnaby told Bob. "Scientists divide Earth into four basic spheres: the **lithosphere,** the **atmosphere,** the **hydrosphere,** and the **biosphere.**

- "The lithosphere includes all the landmasses that make up Earth's crust, such as mountains, plains, and forests.
- "The atmosphere is all the gases that surround Earth.
- "The hydrosphere is all the oceans, lakes, rivers, and other bodies of water that cover more than two-thirds of Earth.
- "And the biosphere is us—all the living things on land, in the air, and in the seas."

"Oh, this is just too awful to bear," Bob said, lowering himself to lie on the couch. "I'm just the last one. That's all. It's okay. Breathe," he told himself, "just breathe."

"You okay, Bob?" Angie asked.

"I'm not great, to be honest. Would you be a dear and bring a glass of water? Oh yes, with a straw maybe," he said holding up his handless wings in explanation. "I'm stuck here. I'll never fall in love. I'll never raise a family. I'll never battle a brontosaurus."

"I thought you were an herbivore," Bridget said, "someone who only eats plants and such."

"Herbivore, shmerbivore, what's it matter anymore?" Bob bemoaned. "We all die alone anyway, right?"

"You have us," Angie said shyly.

"Yes, yes, I do have you dear, little people," Bob said, sarcastically, holding his wing up to his forehead. "How comforting. I can be your pet."

"Earth just isn't a static place," Barnaby continued. "It's constantly changing. The sooner you accept that, the happier you'll be. The fact is that all the continents are broken into separate smaller sections. These separate sections are called **plates,** and they are in constant motion. Plate tectonics is a geological theory that argues that these pieces of the continents are in slow, constant motion because of **convection**—remember that's a heat transfer by the motion of a heat-carrying medium—currents that come up from the mantle. Take a look at this," Barnaby added as he pushed aside his drawing of Earth and began stacking bricks.

TRY IT YOURSELF!

Tectonics

MATERIALS
1 baking pan, 2 candles, 2 candle holders, 8 bricks, 2 sponges, 6 cups of water, 5 pushpins

STEPS
1. Stick the pins into the narrow edge of one of the sponges.
2. Place the bricks in two stacks of four and place the baking pan on top of them. (**Be careful:** Make sure that the bricks support BOTH ends of the pan.)

continued on next page

continued from previous page

3. Fill the pan with a depth of about 2 inches of water.

4. Moisten both sponges so that they float, and then place them side-by-side in the pan of water with the pushpins separating them.

5. Let go of the sponges but make sure they don't float apart.

6. In your *Science Smart Journal,* quickly sketch the positions of both sponges in the pan.

7. With an adult's assistance, carefully light both candles under the pan. Watch closely what happens to the sponges as the water heats.

8. In your *Science Smart Journal,* sketch the positions of both sponges in the pan after 1 minute and then again after 3 minutes.

"So you see that because of the heat rising from inside Earth, the plates move just like the sponges did," Barnaby explained.

"Maybe that's why I can never find anything after I've put it down somewhere," Bridget said. "I mean just the other day I could have sworn that I left my Yankees hat on the rack by the door. But then after looking for like half an hour, I found it under my bed."

"Interesting theory," Barnaby said as Angie came back with Bob's water, "but I don't think so."

"Thank you," Bob said as Angie held the water for him. Bob sipped at it from the straw. "You wouldn't happen to have a wedge of lemon for this would you?"

"Sorry, no," Angie told the dinosaur.

"It'll do then," he sighed. "Everything's all wrong anyway. Why should I expect anything else?"

"The thing about the constant movement of Earth's plates is that it creates **stress,**" Barnaby said.

"Clearly," Bob said.

"Stress on the lithosphere," Barnaby continued, "is a force that can cause rocks to change shape or volume. In extreme cases this stress can cause **earthquakes,** which are the shaking and trembling that result from the movement of rock beneath Earth's surface. It's like this in a way," Barnaby said, pulling a tongue depressor from his coat pocket.

TRY IT YOURSELF!

Stress

MATERIALS
1 tongue depressor

STEPS
1. Slowly bend the tongue depressor into an upside down "U," grasping it by the ends. Stop bending when it looks like the tongue depressor might break.
2. Let go of the tongue depressor. In your *Science Smart Journal*, record what happens to it. Explain why this may be the result.
3. Repeat step 1. This time, though, bend the tongue depressor until both ends touch.
4. In your *Science Smart Journal*, record what happens. Explain why this may be the result.

"This is what can happen when the forces of plate movement bend Earth's crust," Barnaby explained, throwing away the broken depressor. "Depending on the force of the stress, the crust may bend or it may break."

"All is deceit. All is a dream," Bob added, shaking his weary head, his scales tearing the couch fabric. "All is not as it seems."

"You're bringing me down, man," Bridget said.

"I'm bringing *her* down," Bob said to himself, ruefully. "Ah, the folly of youth."

"What's the folly of youth?" Angie asked her brother, tugging at the hem of his lab coat.

"My point exactly," Bob sighed. "What is the folly of youth? I'm in full existential crisis here. Angie, can I have another glass of water?"

"Would you prefer a juice box?" Angie asked. "We have cranberry-apple."

"That would be delightful. Let me gorge myself on sugary drinks. Maybe that will make the days pass more quickly," Bob exclaimed, rather dramatically, rubbing his temples with the ends of his wings. "So you were saying, Barnaby, stress," Bob added.

"There are all different kinds of stress," Barnaby began again. "Stress that pushes sections of rock in opposite directions is called **shearing.** Stress that squeezes a rock until it breaks is called **compression.** And stress that pulls on a rock, stretching it enough to pull it apart, is called **tension.**"

"Does he always prattle on like this?" Bob asked Bridget.

"Yes," she said, grinning, "isn't it amazing?"

"See," Barnaby said, his back to them as he pulled a book down off a shelf. "Check this out."

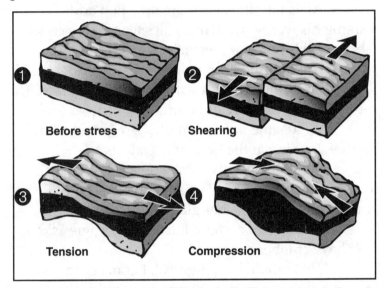

"Not to be rude," Bob said, "but it's not clear to me exactly how any of this information is supposed to make me feel better."

"It's not," Barnaby said, shrugging.

"Delightful. What's next, a lecture on what's inside a hot dog?" Bob asked.

"That," Barnaby told Bob, "you don't want to know."

"Wonderful. Continue then, lad. What's next on the agenda?" Bob said as Angie held his juice box for him.

"Mountain building," Barnaby said, taking a seat on the couch. "Over millions of years, plate movement can transform a flat plain into an enormous mountain range. Mountains are generally created in one of two ways, by folding or by faulting. A **fault** is a break in the lithosphere where slabs of crust slip past each other. There are a number of different types of faults. When two faults occur opposite to each other, it creates a stray segment of rock between the faults. As the wall of each fault slips downward, the rock segment between them moves upward. It's like this," Barnaby said, turning a few more pages in his book.

Mountain Created by Parallel Faults

Normal faults

"Mountains formed by folding, on the other hand," Barnaby continued.

"Must we?" Bob interrupted.

"We must," Barnaby added, and Angie nodded her head "yes" in anxious anticipation of the rest of the explanation. "Have you ever skidded to a stop on a rug that wrinkled under your feet?"

"No, honestly, I can't say I have. My species went extinct, I believe, before the invention of carpet."

"Angie, then," Barnaby asked, "would you do the honors?" Without being asked again, Angie sprinted to the front hall, leapt to a stop on the throw rug in front of the front door, and the rug wrinkled underfoot. "And just like that rug, rocks under compression may bend but not break. Plate collisions can cause just such compression, which in turn causes the world's grandest mountain ranges.

"How *very* thrilling," said Bob, deadpan.

"Sometimes Earth's changes can be deadly. Take, for instance, the case of **volcanoes.** Volcanoes are weak spots in the crust of Earth, where a molten mixture of rock, gas, and water vapor—also known as **magma**—can break through to the surface."

"I thought that when volcanoes erupt," Angie said, "they spew **lava,** not magma."

"You are correct," Barnaby told his sister, tussling her hair, which prompted Bob to groan in disdain. "When magma reaches the surface, we call it lava. Check this out," Barnaby said, pulling a book about volcanos off the shelf.

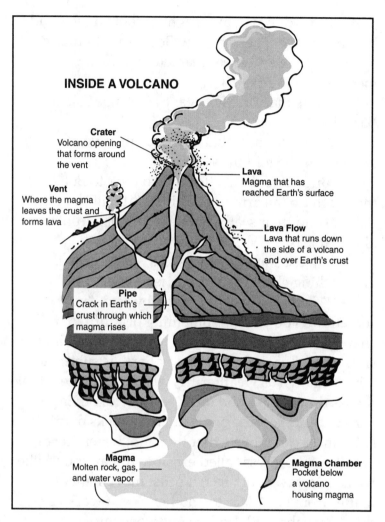

INSIDE A VOLCANO

Crater
Volcano opening
that forms around
the vent

Lava
Magma that has
reached Earth's surface

Vent
Where the magma
leaves the crust and
forms lava

Lava Flow
Lava that runs down
the side of a volcano
and over Earth's crust

Pipe
Crack in Earth's
crust through which
magma rises

Magma
Molten rock, gas,
and water vapor

Magma Chamber
Pocket below
a volcano
housing magma

"There's just no point, is there? Life is short, brutish, and cruel," Bob said, standing up onto his hind legs, bumping his head against the ceiling, and then plodding carefully over to the window. "Why me? Why me?" he sighed wistfully, staring out across the front yard. A passing neighbor looked over and began to wave. Then she saw Bob's snout pushed against a pane and she screamed and ran away instead.

"Was that Dr. McSweeney?" Angie asked Barnaby.

"I'd recognize that bloodcurdling yelp anywhere," he told his sister.

Bridget and Babette walked over to Bob, and they each put an arm around him. "It will be okay," Babette told their scaly friend. "I promise. You're not alone, at least."

"It just sounds so hopeless," Bob wailed. "Everything changes. Nothing is forever."

"That may be true," Barnaby said, "but sometimes you can get something beautiful out of change. Because of changes in temperature, rain, ice, snow, and the wind, the crust of Earth is subject to what's known as **weathering,** which is a process that breaks down rocks and other substances on Earth's surface. And because of weathering, rocks or other substances can move either by wind, water, ice, or gravity in a process called **erosion.** It may sound like wearing away, but in fact, it's just movement of matter from one place to another. See, it works like this," Barnaby said, leading everyone into the kitchen.

Try It Yourself!

Erosion

Materials
tape, pen, 3 paper cups, water, mud, aluminum pan, ruler

Steps
1. Form the mud into 3 golf ball-shaped figures. Allow the mud to dry for an hour.
2. Label three cups "1," "2," and "3."
3. Using your pen, poke 6 to 8 holes around the bottom edge of Cup 1.
4. Using your pen, poke 10 to 12 holes in the bottom of Cup 2.
5. Fill Cup 3 with water.
6. In your *Science Smart Journal* note the approximate diameter and shape of the dried mud "golf balls."
7. Secure the ruler standing up to the side of Cup 1. Place Cup 1 in the center of the aluminum pan. Place a mud ball in the cup.
8. Holding Cup 2 four to five inches above Cup 1, pour the water from Cup 3 into Cup 2.

Cup 1

continued on next page

continued from previous page

9. After all the water has drained out into the aluminum pan, study what happened to the mud ball. Record your observations in your *Science Smart Journal.*

10. Repeat steps 5–9 with the other two mud balls. Note the differences if any.

"See," Barnaby said as he cleaned his hands in the sink. "The pouring water eroded the mud like a rainstorm might. The movement of the dirt into the pan is erosion. And the dirt in the pan is called **sediment,** which is any small, solid particles from rocks or organisms that are moved by water or wind."

"I think I can feel myself eroding," Bob said, touching his face gently.

"You're losing it, man," Bridget told her dinosaur friend.

"Precisely," Bob sighed, "I *am* losing it. In fact, I'm worse than losing it. I've lost it. I need to lie down," he added, slumping onto the kitchen floor and rolling onto his back. His legs were up in the air, and his wings unfurled so that they stretched practically the whole width of the kitchen.

"Erosion can be beautiful, though. All the rivers in the world are the products of thousands, maybe millions, of years of erosion. Mountains, plateaus, peaks, valleys, deltas, and plains are all the result of some form of erosion. We wouldn't have the Grand Canyon without the process of erosion. It's not a bad thing. It's just change," Barnaby said.

"I'd just like to stop changing for a moment, if you don't mind," Bob sighed. "It's getting awfully hard to keep up."

"I understand," Angie told Bob. She lay down next to him and put her arms around the sad dinosaur's neck. "Don't worry, Bob. We'll take care of you. I promise."

"That's nice," Bob said. "Maybe I just need a nap. Maybe I'll wake up and it'll be the Mesozoic age again."

And just then, the doorbell rang. Barnaby, Bridget, and Babette all looked at each other. They weren't expecting another pizza and Barnaby's parents wouldn't ring the bell unless they'd lost their keys or something. The three of them went to the front door together. "Who's there?" Barnaby asked, as he'd been taught to do, before answering the door.

"It's Mr. and Dr. McSweeney, Barnaby. Please open up," a voice outside said.

The blood rushed from all three of their faces. "Uh," Barnaby stuttered, "what do you want?"

"We just wanted to, uh, check up on you," Dr. McSweeney said. "Make sure everything's okay."

"We're not supposed to open the door for strangers," Bridget said a bit too quickly.

"We're not strangers," Mr. McSweeney cut in. "We're your neighbors. Have been for years. We work at the university with your parents. You know that."

"It's nothing really, Barnaby," Dr. McSweeney said. "It's just I could have sworn I saw . . . "

"Uh, we're fine," Barnaby interrupted, and then turning to Bridget and Babette, he whispered, "They want Bob."

"Duh," Bridget said. "What do we do?"

"We cannot let them find him," Babette said. "They will want to lock him up in a zoo."

"Or worse, they might want to do all sorts of painful tests on him," Bridget added.

"We have to get him out of here," Barnaby added.

"Son, please open the door," Mr. McSweeney said again.

"Uh, um, let me just, uh, get decent," Barnaby mumbled back, heading back to the kitchen.

"Get decent?" Bridget asked.

"I saw it in a movie once," Barnaby added as the McSweeneys began banging on the door. "Bob!" Barnaby screamed as they got into the kitchen. "Get up."

"Do I have to?" Bob sighed. "What's the point really? We all inevitably end up in this position. Effort is a pointless dream of the vain."

"The McSweeneys are at the front door," Bridget said.

Babette finished her point by adding, "And they are looking for you."

"And?" Bob asked.

"And Dr. McSweeney works in the University—as a paleontologist she might want to put you in one of their crazy fossil studies. Who knows?" Barnaby nearly yelled.

"Oh goodness," Bob said, sitting up, "but I haven't done anything wrong."

"You're a dinosaur," Barnaby said. "That's reason enough."

"They can't take Bob," Angie said, standing up and bearing her fists. Barnaby had to grab her by the waist to keep her from charging the front door.

"We have to get out of here," Bob said, dancing on his hind feet as if he were stepping on coals. "What do we do?"

"What do we do?" Bridget asked back to Bob. "You can fly, right?"

"Of course," Bob said as the knocks on the front door grow louder.

"Well then it's time to get to it," Bridget said as all four children climbed up onto Bob's back.

Just as Dr. McSweeney was about to pound on the door again, Bob crashed through the kitchen wall, and with Barnaby, Bridget, Angie, and Babette on his back, he flew off into the atmosphere. "Oh my," Mr. McSweeney said, looking up as the dinosaur and the four kids disappeared into the night sky.

TRY IT YOURSELF!

Volcanoes form in a number of different ways. One type of volcano is called a hot spot volcano. When magma melts through Earth's crust, the area it melts through becomes a hot spot. Hot spots can often be found in the middle of the lithosphere's plates. Hot spot volcanoes can even occur on the ocean floor, where they can gradually form volcanic mountains from hardened magma. The Hawaiian Islands, for instance, were created when the Pacific plate passed over a hot spot. Using your knowledge of hot spot volcanoes, do the experiment on the next page and think about whether it is a good model for hot spot volcanoes.

Hawaii's Hot Spot

continued on next page

continued from previous page

Make Your Own Volcano

MATERIALS
1 deep clear mixing bowl or deep pot, 1 small, empty glass or plastic bottle, water, red food dye, moist sponge

STEPS
1. Fill a deep bowl or pot half full with cool water.
2. Float a sponge on top of the water.
3. Pour a mixture of red food dye and hot (but not boiling) water into an empty bottle.
4. While covering the opening of the bottle with your hand, place the bottle right side up in the bowl or pot of water. The bottle opening must be underwater.
5. Take your hand off the bottle opening.
6. In your *Science Smart Journal*, report what happened. Why is this a good model for what might happen to magma before it becomes lava?

Match each word in the column below with its correct meaning in the column on the next pages.

1. Magma   _____
2. Geosphere   _____
3. Mantle   _____
4. Volcanoes   _____
5. Tension   _____
6. Sediment   _____
7. Hydrosphere   _____
8. Erosion   _____
9. Plates   _____
10. Shearing   _____
11. Earthquake   _____
12. Lithosphere   _____
13. Atmosphere   _____
14. Core   _____
15. Weathering   _____
16. Crust   _____
17. Compression   _____
18. Lava   _____
19. Fault   _____
20. Biosphere   _____
21. Stress   _____

A. A force that can cause rock to change shape or volume
B. The shaking and trembling that can result from the movement of rock beneath Earth's surface
C. The hot, yet solid, layer between Earth's core and crust
D. The movement of rocks or rock particles by wind, water, ice, or gravity
E. Any small, solid particles from rocks or organisms that are moved by water, wind, or glaciers
F. A molten mixture of rock, gas, and water vapor that makes up part of Earth's mantle
G. All the water masses that cover Earth
H. Contains the lithosphere, hydrosphere, and atmosphere (rock and soil, water, and air)
I. Separate sections of Earth's lithosphere
J. Stress that pushes a rock in opposite directions
K. The layer of gases that surrounds Earth
L. A break in the lithosphere at which slabs of crust slip past each other
M. The thin outer surface of Earth
N. Stress that pulls on a rock, stretching it enough to pull it apart
O. Living organisms and their environment
P. Weak spots in the crust of Earth where magma comes to the surface
Q. Stress that squeezes rock until it breaks

R. The outer part of Earth's crust and mantle
S. The process that breaks down the rock and other substances on Earth's surface both physically and chemically
T. The dense center of Earth
U. A molten mixture of rock, gas, and water vapor that has reached Earth's surface

Chapter 10
The Hydrosphere and Atmosphere

Bob was careful to fly slowly. With the wind blowing in the dark sky, it was dangerous up in the air. Besides, he didn't have much experience being airborne, much less with four kids on his back and the staff of the paleontology department hot on his trail. Barnaby was having trouble holding on, and he was trying to pretend that he doesn't get motion sickness. Angie, in her enthusiasm to see what was happening below, could barely keep herself from falling off the side. Babette was, of course, blasé, and Bridget was upset that now she'd never know how the Yankees game ended.

"Look," Angie said, pointing, "I think I see my school. Hello, Mr. Bergman," she hollered, "My homework won't be finished Monday!"

"Do you think," Bridget cut in, "we could circle over Yankee Stadium? We'd have better views than if we were in the blimp."

"Dare I ask: Are you comparing me to a blimp, young lady?" Bob asked.

"This is like a movie," Babette interrupted. "I did not know America would be so much fun."

"I don't feel so good," Barnaby groaned, clutching his stomach. "Can't we just land for a little while?"

"Not just yet," Bob said. "We need a plan first. At least the air up here is helping me clear my head a bit."

"In fact," Barnaby added, "the **atmosphere,** the layer of gases that surround Earth, is thinner up here. As you go up into the atmosphere, the **air density,** the mass of a given volume of air, is less than it is closer to Earth."

"Well, I do feel better. Lighter almost," Bob continued.

"Well, that part isn't surprising, at least. The air density is lower, so the air pressure is too. Bob, please fly as still as possible. Angie," Barnaby said, pulling some books and four balls of clay out of a pocket, "help me with a quick experiment."

TRY IT YOURSELF!

There's Air Up There

MATERIALS
4 books, wax paper, 4 balls of clay

STEPS
1. Place a piece of wax paper on a table, and then place a ball of clay on top of the wax paper.
2. Place another piece of wax paper on top of the clay, and then balance a book on top of that wax paper.
3. Repeat steps 1 and 2 on top of the first book, alternating wax paper, clay, wax paper, and a book. Stack all four books and balls of clay on top of each other.
4. One by one, remove the books and wax paper.
5. In your *Science Smart Journal,* describe the shape of each ball of clay. What differences do you see? How can you account for these differences?

"So you see," Barnaby said as he accidentally dropped a ball of clay off Bob's back as he was putting them away, "each book is like another layer of atmosphere. The air pressure is highest closest to Earth because there are heavy layers of atmosphere on top of it. In fact, there are actually four layers of atmosphere. The **troposphere** is the lowest layer, closest to Earth. It's where clouds form and weather occurs. The **stratosphere** is the next level. It's where the ozone layer lies. Some high-flying airplanes make it up into the lower stratosphere. Next is my personal favorite."

"You have a personal favorite?" Bridget asked, incredulous.

"Of course, doesn't everyone?" Barnaby said, shrugging. "It's the **mesosphere.** It's about sixty kilometers from the surface of Earth. We transmit some radio waves from here to avoid things like mountains that might block transmission. And last and biggest, of course, is the lonely **thermosphere.** The thermosphere extends over five hundred kilometers in altitude. Beyond the thermosphere is outside our atmosphere, which is known colloquially as outer space."

"My goodness, I've never heard someone your age use a word like 'colloquially' in polite conversation," Bob cut in. "It means, commonly, right?"

"I'm older than you," Barnaby said defiantly.

"I suppose you are," Bob said, "but then I'm extinct, so I outrank you regardless. Guys," Bob said, changing tone, "what do you think the paleontologists will do to me if they catch me?"

"They're not going to catch you," Bridget told Bob, hugging him tight. "We won't let them."

"I can't be a display in some museum. I don't deal well with being stared at," Bob said as he began to cry. "I'm not a bad guy. I don't deserve this."

"You're a great guy," Angie said.

"You are the best," Babette agreed. "You are a regular Emil Zola."

"E-mail what-a?" Bridget asked.

"Do you guys know anything about history? Emil Zola was one of the greatest heroes of freedom in French history. Just like Bob. Look it up."

"Guys," Barnaby interrupted, "I'm sorry, but we gotta land. I'm going to be sick."

"But where?" Bridget said. "It's too risky."

"I know just the place," Angie said, whispering into Bob's ear. He took a hard turn right, nearly losing Bridget in the process, and minutes later Bob landed in the fossil garden of the City Natural History Museum and Observatory, which had closed for the day. Barnaby leapt off Bob's back and threw up back by the picnic tables. The rest of the kids checked the area to make sure it was safe. "No one will think to look for us in the one place they want to put us," Angie said proudly.

"Put *me*, you mean," Bob said, turning to see a life-sized tyrannosaurus skeleton staring back at him. He jumped back startled, a wing to his chest, gasping for a breath. "That's just horrifying. You people pay to look at this?"

"It's science," Angie told him. "It's the only evidence we have to study."

"It's twisted," Bob said, stepping over to where a stegosaurus skeleton stood. "I think I knew him," Bob added.

"You did not," Angie sighed. "They were dead long before you were born."

"Thank you," Bob said, nodding, "that makes me feel so much better."

"Babette and I will take a quick trip around to make sure that everything is safe and to see if maybe we can find a good place to hide," Bridget offered. "In the meantime, Barnaby, why don't you tell Angie more about all that atmosphere stuff you were talking about before?"

"Excellent idea," Barnaby said as Angie jumped up and down, clapping her hands in excitement.

"More science talk," Bob said. "Terrific."

"Would you be impressed if I made you a cloud?" Barnaby asked.

"You can do that?" Angie asked, eyes widening.

"Easy," Barnaby said, taking an empty soda bottle out of the garbage before sliding through an opening in the back door to enter the concession stand in the museum.

TRY IT YOURSELF!

Clouds

MATERIALS
1 empty soda bottle, 35 ml hot water,
1 ice cube

STEPS
1. Pour about 35 ml of hot water into the empty soda bottle.
2. Rest the ice cube on the top of the open bottle.
3. Record your observations in your *Science Smart Journal*.

"That's so cool," Angie said, marveling at the small cloud that had formed at the top of the bottle. "But I don't understand how they form in real life."

"Don't you see," Bob sighed, throwing up his wings, "we're trapped in that bottle too, metaphorically speaking. We're all stuck on this tiny speck of a planet, this miserable celestial experiment with no end in sight. There's no escape," he added, walking over a brontosaurus fossil, "and some day we all end up in a garden being gawked at by school children with hands that are stained orange from too many cheese puffs. I'm going to lie down," Bob added as he sprawled out on the grass.

"Right here?" Barnaby asked.

"What's the difference," Bob said. "It's futile to get up."

"Suit yourself," Barnaby said, "but to answer your question, Angie, weather is greatly affected by one of Earth's most abundant substances: water. In fact, the **water cycle** provides the basis for Earth's weather. See," Barnaby said, making a quick sketch on the sidewalk with a lost piece of chalk.

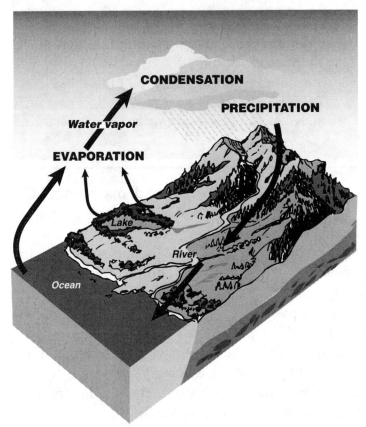

"You see," Barnaby explained, "the water cycle is a way that water moves from Earth's surface into the atmosphere and then back to Earth's surface. It moves from Earth's surface from bodies of water, land, and living things into the atmosphere in a process called **evaporation.** Evaporation happens when water absorbs enough energy from the Sun to turn from a liquid into a gas, **water vapor.** It's sort of like the steam you might see coming off a cup of coffee, except it occurs more slowly and invisibly. Clouds form when water floats high into the atmosphere. Why? Because up there the temperature is much cooler and the water vapor condenses back into plain ol' liquid water. The water then clumps together around dust particles in the air to form clouds. As more and more water clumps around the dust, it grows heavier and heavier until it falls back to Earth. Water that falls to Earth as hail, sleet, snow, or rain is called **precipitation.**"

"Yes," Bob said, groaning through his double-set of teeth, "let's talk about the weather. How droll?"

"But really it's all about the **humidity,**" Barnaby said, pushing forward with his line of thought regardless.

"What is?" Angie wanted to know.

"Often it's the humidity that makes us uncomfortable on hot summer days. Humidity is the amount of water vapor in the air. You see the air is like, well, my hair in a way. Water sticks in it and stays— just like things in my hair. See, check this out," he added, pulling a metal container out of the garbage.

TRY IT YOURSELF!

It's So Humid

MATERIALS

1 empty soup can with the label removed, room temperature water, ice cubes, thermometer, pencil

STEPS

1. Tape the thermometer to the inside of the can so that you can easily read the temperature.
2. Fill the can halfway with water.
3. Stir the water slowly, carefully adding one ice cube at a time.
4. Observe the outside of the container closely. Note the temperature at which moisture begins forming on the outside of the can.
5. Record that temperature in your *Science Smart Journal.*
6. Repeat steps 1–3 three more times. Before each trial make sure to wipe the outside of the can dry. Find the average temperature for the three trials. Explain where you think the water came from, what may have happened to the air around the container, and why the water appeared when it did.

"It's just like we discussed earlier with solutions," Barnaby explained. "When the air around the container became **saturated,** which occurs when it can't hold any more moisture, water vapor condensed on the outside of the container. The temperature at which this happens, when water vapor becomes liquid, is called the **dew point.** On humid summer days the air temperature is at or above the dew point. When something changes from a gas to a liquid it's called **condensation.** So water can condense out of the air onto anything it can find, like your skin."

"Ah, yes, life is an endless circle, sort of like your water cycle," Bob said. "I am condemned forever to be the last of an extinct breed. Can you imagine what that feels like?" Bob added, the scales on the back of his neck standing on end.

"You know, Bob," Angie told the dinosaur, "if you hadn't gotten lost in Barnaby's hair, we wouldn't have ever met you. Don't you think every cloud has a silver lining?"

"In fact, clouds don't have silver linings at all," Barnaby told his sister.

"You always have to be so literal," Angie complained, hugging herself to keep warm. She was only in her pajamas and the sun had already set, so she was starting to feel very cold.

Bob noticed Angie's teeth starting to chatter. "Dear girl," he said, "you seem positively frozen. Don't you own a sweater?"

"Yes," she said shyly. "At home."

"Oh goodness, come here," Bob responded. Angie snuggled under his wing, tightly against his side. "Barnaby, can't you do something to warm us up?"

"Since the Sun has already set," Barnaby explained, taking his hands out of his pockets for the moment, "there's not much I can really do. The Sun's rays heat Earth."

"How does it work?" asked Angie, trying to imagine the Sun's rays keeping her warm.

Barnaby responded, "Energy from the Sun's rays does many things when it reaches Earth. Some of it is absorbed by the land and water, and some actually is reflected, which means that it bounces off of the surface of Earth. However, even when the energy in the Sun's rays is reflected back toward space, water vapor, methane, carbon dioxide, and other gases in the air usually absorb it before it gets back out to space. This absorbed energy heats the gases in the air. The gases then form a blanket around Earth, trapping the heat near the surface of the planet. The process by which gases hold heat in the air is called the **greenhouse effect.** There's a very simple experiment to demonstrate," Barnaby added, fishing two empty soup bowls out of the garbage.

TRY IT YOURSELF!

The Greenhouse Effect

MATERIALS

2 identical bowls, soil, 2 thermometers, plastic wrap, pen, clock with second hand

Greenhouse Data Time (minutes)					
Container	At start	15	30	45	60
Covered bowl					
Uncovered bowl					

STEPS

1. Copy the chart above into your *Science Smart Journal*.
2. Cover the bottom of each bowl with about 6 inches of soil.
3. Place a thermometer on top of the soil in each bowl.
4. Cover one bowl with plastic wrap.
5. Record the initial temperature readings in your *Science Smart Journal*.

continued on next page

continued from previous page

6. Place both bowls next to each other outside in the sun.
7. Every 15 minutes for 1 hour, record the temperature readings from both thermometers in your _Science Smart Journal._

"Okay, so it's not really an experiment that we can do with much success now," Barnaby explained, tapping the side of one of the thermometers, "but I swear it'll work when the sun comes out."

Just then, stealing from between the displays, Bridget and Babette returned. "The McSweeneys are at the front gate," Bridget said, breathlessly. "And they've brought the rest of the science faculty with them."

"We'd better get a move on," Babette told them all.

"Get a move on?" Barnaby said, mocking her.

"I watch a lot of cop movies. What is your problem?" Babette responded.

"Can this wait until later?" Bob asked anxiously. "We had better find a better hiding place fast before any of us—myself especially—find themselves suddenly fossilized."

"The observatory," Bridget told them without explanation.

"It's the perfect hiding place," Babette said. "No one is there, and the door is unlocked."

"Perfect," Barnaby said, "let's head out."

"Let's get where it's warm," Angie chimed in.

"Yeah, what happened to the weather?" Bridget asked, rubbing her hands together then blowing into them. "It was warm two days ago."

"Funny you should ask," Barnaby said, but Bob cut in. "Barnaby!" Bob yelled in his scariest dinosaur tone. "If you're going to give us a lecture, do it while you're running please. We're in a bit of a rush, wouldn't you say?"

"Fair enough," Barnaby nodded, hefting Angie up onto his shoulders as he picked up the pace just to keep up. "The greenhouse effect helps keep energy— heat—close to Earth's surface. But yet, as we all know, weather changes daily. The changes are caused by the movement of large air masses, which are bodies of air with properties determined by where the air mass develops. Air masses that develop over the Sahara Desert will be drier than air masses that develop over the Indian Ocean. Air masses that develop over Cuba will be warmer than ones that develop over Alaska. Air masses move constantly," Barnaby explained, spinning around in front of the group as they walked, "and when two air masses collide," he added clapping Angie's hands together for her, "they form a front. If we weren't in such a rush, I know the perfect little experiment to demonstrate," he told his friends slowly as he had to catch his breath between explanations.

TRY IT YOURSELF!

Fronting

MATERIALS

1 shoe box-sized plastic container, 1 plastic divider, water, blue food coloring, red food coloring, salt

STEPS

1. Insert the plastic divider tightly in the middle of the container. (It should fit snuggly enough that water cannot seep through.)
2. Pour warm water on the left side of the divider and cold water on the right side.
3. Add red food dye to the left (warm) side of the divider.
4. Add blue food dye and about 100 ml of salt to the right (cold) side of the divider.
5. Remove the divider carefully but quickly.
6. Record your observations in your *Science Smart Journal.* Be sure to observe what is happening from the side of the box as well as from above.

"The point is," Barnaby continued, "because cold air is denser, it falls to the bottom when air masses collide. Like I said before, that's what creates a front. There are four types of fronts: *cold fronts, warm fronts, stationary fronts,* and *occluded fronts.* A cold front forms when cold air moves underneath warm air, forcing the warm air to rise."

COLD FRONT

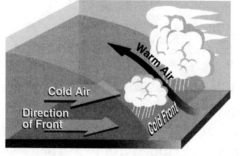

"A warm front, on the other hand, occurs when the warm air moves over the cold air," Barnaby continued.

WARM FRONT

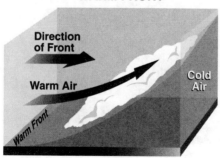

"A stationary front occurs when neither the cold air or the warm air move. Precipitation sometimes forms along the front between the air masses," Barnaby added.

STATIONARY FRONT

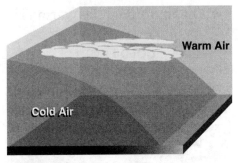

"And lastly, on occasion, two cold air masses may come together, trapping warm air between them. The result is an occluded front," Barnaby said, running out of breath as he jogged up the hill to the observatory.

OCCLUDED FRONT

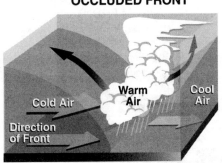

Dr. McSweeney stopped at the foot of the hill that the observatory sat atop as Bridget laid into the front door, popping it open, and Barnaby let Angie down off his shoulders. "Barnaby, Angie," Dr. McSweeney said into a megaphone, "we're not here to hurt anyone. I'm here with the rest of the paleontology department. We just want to take a close look at your friend, Mr. Dinosaur."

"She's so patronizing," Angie harrumphed to Barnaby.

The five of them scurried safely inside, closing the door behind them. "Safe for now," Bridget sighed as she locked the door, pulling out the key that was left in the dead bolt and stuffing it deep in her pocket.

"We should give ourselves up," Bob said. "I can't bear the thought of getting you kids in trouble."

"Look, there's got to be a better solution," Barnaby said as he began to pace. "We just need to think."

"Think about what?" a voice said from a darkened hallway.

"I thought you said this place was empty!" Angie yelled, nearly hysterical.

"I thought it was. All the lights were off," Bridget said.

"The lights are off," the voice said, coming out into the entryway. "Dear me, I'm sorry," he said, tapping his cane on the stone floor. "It doesn't make sense to waste electricity on the light when you're blind."

"Professor Jimenez?" Barnaby said.

"Barnaby, is that you?" the professor asked.

"Yes, it's me. I had no idea you were up here," Barnaby said. "Professor Jimenez is one of the most brilliant astrophysicists in the world."

"Oh, you're too kind," he said. "Don't stop."

"He used to work at the university with Mom and Dad," Barnaby said. "Until . . . "

"They forced me to retire," Professor Jimenez added, finishing Barnaby's thought. "Who are your friends?"

"Well, this is my sister, Angie, and my friends Babette and Bridget," Barnaby said, purposefully ignoring Bob. The girls introduced themselves, but Professor Jimenez was confused.

"I could have sworn that I heard another voice," he said.

"Oh, uh, that, um, that was Bob," Barnaby said.

"Bob," the professor said, extending a hand, "it's a pleasure." And since no one could think fast enough, Bob extended a wing and shook the professor's hand. "You should use moisturizer, son," the professor whispered. "It works wonders."

And just as the professor was about to show them around, Dr. McSweeney interrupted again. "We have the observatory surrounded. There's no escape," she said. "Come out with your hands up."

Everybody froze. "Barnaby," Professor Jimenez said, "would you care to explain?"

"It's a long story," Barnaby sighed.

"Well, I've got time to listen," the professor said, taking a careful seat on an empty box. After a deep breath, Barnaby told the professor the best lie he could come up with.

Reading a Weather Map

Many newspapers print weather maps to give their readers an easy way to read about the day's weather. Examine the weather map below, and use the information on it to answer questions 1–3.

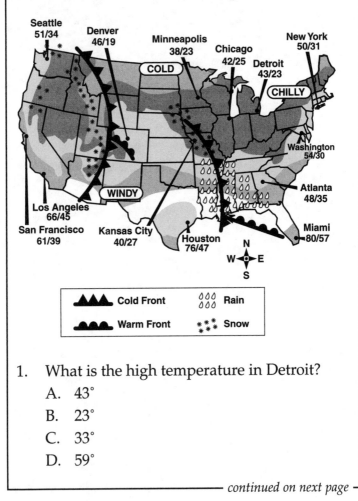

1. What is the high temperature in Detroit?

    A. 43°

    B. 23°

    C. 33°

    D. 59°

continued on next page

— continued from previous page —

2. A storm system heads east from Kansas City. The forecast calls for snow in Chicago but rain in Atlanta. What is the *most likely* explanation for why it would be snowing in Chicago but raining in Atlanta?

    A. There are two separate cold fronts.
    B. Snow often turns to rain after a while.
    C. The temperature is higher in Atlanta than in Chicago.
    D. Chicago is on a lake whereas Atlanta is land bound.

3. In your *Science Smart Journal,* track the weather reports in your local newspaper for a week. Look carefully for patterns: when it rains, when it snows, when it's warmer or colder. The next week, without looking at the newspaper predictions, try to make your own weather predictions. See how close you were to being correct and note why you're predictions proved right or wrong.

Matching

Match each word in the column below with its correct meaning in the column on the next pages.

1. Mesosphere   _____

2. Precipitation   _____

3. Front   _____

4. Saturated   _____

5. Thermosphere   _____

6. Water cycle   _____

7. Greenhouse effect   _____

8. Water vapor   _____

9. Troposphere   _____

10. Dew point   _____

11. Humidity   _____

12. Stratosphere   _____

13. Evaporation   _____

14. Air masses   _____

15. Atmosphere   _____

16. Air density   _____

A. The process through which water moves from bodies of water, land, and living things on Earth's surface into the atmosphere and then back down to Earth's surface
B. Water in its gaseous state
C. The atmospheric layer in which the ozone layer lies
D. The temperature at which condensation happens
E. The atmospheric layer extending from eighty to over five hundred kilometers in altitude
F. The layer of gases that surrounds Earth
G. The process by which water absorbs enough energy from the Sun to turn from a liquid to a gaseous state
H. The area at which two air masses collide
I. Water that falls to Earth as hail, sleet, snow, or rain
J. The amount of water vapor in the air
K. The process by which gases in the atmosphere trap solar radiation and keep it near a planet's surface

L. The atmospheric layer where some radio waves are transmitted

M. The state at which something can't hold any more material in it

N. Bodies of air with properties determined by the part of Earth's surface over which they develop

O. The atmospheric layer in which clouds form and weather occurs

P. The mass of a given volume of air

Chapter 11
Earth and the Solar System

"Well that is quite a problem," Professor Jimenez replied, stroking his goatee, as Barnaby finished his story. "I have trouble believing, though, that the whole faculty of the university's paleontology department is after poor Angie simply because she didn't complete her homework. And, besides, what's she doing studying at the university? Your sister can't be more than six years old."

"I'm eight," Angie said, stomping her feet defiantly.

"And she's a genius," Bridget interrupted. "It was more than just homework too. She was doing some very important research for them."

"Really now?" the professor said, still clearly unconvinced. "What kind of research was that then?"

"They, uh, wanted her to find the last living dinosaur," Babette blurted out.

"Oh you're kidding me," the professor sighed, shaking his head. "Dr. McSweeney hasn't given up on that ridiculous idea?"

"Oh no, she's taking it quite seriously," Barnaby said.

"She's a crackpot," the professor added. "She used to think that there was an opening under your house, Barnaby and Angie, to a kind of alternative, prehistoric world. Your parents wouldn't let her within 100 feet of the place. She'd perform all sorts of painful laboratory tests on the poor animals."

"That's barbaric," Bob said.

"That it is. I told her that once," the professor added, smiling, "and that's why I ended up here."

"It's not so bad here," Angie said as she scanned the bare walls and rock floors that decorated the aging observatory. There was a plaque in the corner that said it was built in 1959. Judging from the spider webs in the corners and the layer of dust on every tabletop, Angie figured it hadn't been cleaned since then.

"It's a dump," the professor said, "but it's home. So what are we going to do about the crazy professors? They said they were going to go fetch the police."

"Maybe they'll forget," Angie suggested.

"Oh, I doubt that," Professor Jimenez said. "They're a tough bunch. They'll camp out for the evening if they want something you have," he added, moving to rustle Angie's hair. Instead he ended up mussing the petals of some fresh-cut flowers in a vase. "I'll make you a deal. You help me set up an experiment that I've been working on, and I'll show you a secret exit out of here."

"Deal," Barnaby agreed quickly, without bothering to consult his friends.

"Now, tell me kids, how much do you know about Earth and the Solar System?" When no one said a word, the professor sighed and shook his head again. Carefully, he headed toward his telescope and said, "Well, c'mon, let's learn something. Take a seat in front of the telescope. I'll be back in a second," he said.

"Barnaby," Bridget said as soon as the professor was out of earshot, "we can't sit here and listen to him lecture us about the Solar System."

"I know, I know," Barnaby said. "But let's let the old guy talk for a little while and, hopefully, he'll show us the secret exit."

"But what about Dr. McSweeney?" Babette asked. "She wants to torture Bob."

"Must you put it that way?" Bob asked pleadingly.

"Are you sure they can't get in?" Angie said. "What if they really get the police?"

"Bridget," Barnaby asked, "do you still have the key?"

"Sure do," she said, showing it to everyone.

"Then we're safe for a little while at least," Barnaby nodded.

"Good, good," the professor interrupted then, as he carried a tray full of cookies and glasses of milk. "I put together a little something for you."

"Oh goodness," Babette said, jumping to her feet, "do you need help?"

"I'm blind, not clumsy," he said, setting the tray in front of the kids and Bob. "Help yourself." They all grabbed cookies, except Bob, who couldn't because he didn't have hands. Angie had to help him, and she could barely contain her laughter when Bob wound up with a milk mustache. "So," the professor said, quieting everyone down, "let's start our discussion with the **inner planets:** Mercury, Venus, Earth, and Mars. The inner planets are relatively small, and they all have rocky surfaces. See here," he said, pulling down a map hung on the far wall that showed all the inner planets of the Solar System.

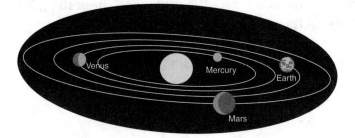

"**Mercury,**" Professor Jimenez continued, "is the closest planet to the Sun. It's also the second smallest planet in the Solar System. It's not much bigger than our Moon. **Venus** is next in line. It's similar to Earth in size, density, and internal structure. However, it's also pretty different from Earth. For instance, it has a very slow rotation; a day on Venus is equal to a year on Earth. After that, of course, there's good old Mother **Earth.** Her surface is seventy percent water. No other planet has oceans like Earth does. The farthest of the inner planets is **Mars.** It has a slightly reddish tinge and about one percent the gravitational pressure of Earth. Mars also has two very small moons, Phobos and Deimos."

"I always wanted to go to Mars," Barnaby interrupted.

"To meet Martians girls," Angie said, making kissing noises at her brother.

"No," he said, giving her a playful shove. "To try to discover proof of intelligent life in the universe."

"You mean you can't find any intelligent life on Earth," Babette joked.

"Clearly," Barnaby said, winking at Babette.

"Regardless," Professor Jimenez continued, "just like there are inner planets, so, too, are there **outer planets.** There are five outer planets: Jupiter, Saturn, Uranus, Neptune, and Pluto. See here," he added, pulling down another map.

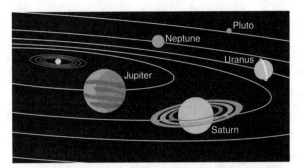

"Jupiter, Saturn, Uranus, and Neptune are far bigger than Earth, and they don't have solid surfaces," the professor continued. "**Jupiter** is the most massive planet in our Solar System. It's made up of mostly hydrogen and helium. It has a huge red spot on its surface, coincidentally called the 'Great Red Spot,' which is an ongoing storm similar to a hurricane. The Great Red Spot, believe it or not, is many times bigger than Earth. **Saturn** is the second largest planet. It has rings around it made of chunks of ice and rock. Saturn is the only planet less dense than water. **Uranus** is about four times the size of Earth. It looks bluish to the eye because of traces of methane in its atmosphere. Uranus wasn't discovered until 1781. **Neptune** is the eighth planet from the Sun. It's about thirty times farther from the Sun than Earth is. Neptune was discovered after Uranus, because astronomers noticed that something was affecting Uranus's orbit. And finally there's little baby **Pluto**. Pluto wasn't discovered until 1930. It's the only planet in our Solar System that we haven't visited with spacecraft. It's different than the other outer planets in that it has a solid surface and a mass less than that of Earth. Pluto is so far from the Sun that a year on Pluto, one full revolution around the Sun, is the same as 248 years on Earth."

"Wow," Barnaby cut in, "that's even older than you are."

"Not by much, unfortunately," the professor laughed. "Actually, that gives me an idea. How about a quick demonstration to show how the distance from the Sun is related to the time needed to complete a revolution?"

TRY IT YOURSELF!

Around and Around

MATERIALS
2 m string, meter stick, 6 small washers, stopwatch, 1 eraser, Phillips-head screwdriver, 1 straw

STEPS
1. In your *Science Smart Journal,* recreate the table on the next page.

continued on next page

— continued from previous page —

Data Table

Period of Revolution (seconds)			
Distance (cm)	Trial 1	Trial 2	Trial 3	Average
30				
60				
90				

2. With an adult supervising, make a hole in the center of the eraser with the screwdriver.

3. Thread the string through the hole in your eraser and tie the end to the main part of the string. Pull the knot tight so that the eraser will not fly loose.

4. Pull the string through the straw, and then thread it through the 6 washers; tie the string around the washers. The washers should keep the string from slipping out of the straw.

5. Holding the straw, practice slowly swinging the eraser over your head like a lasso. Try to get it going at a constant speed. Be careful to conduct your experiment in an empty room away from people or breakables.

— continued on next page —

6. Measure 30 cm from the end of the straw to the eraser. Secure the washers close to the bottom of the straw so the length of string remains 30 cm.

7. Swing the eraser just fast enough to keep it moving. Have a partner time how long it takes to make 10 revolutions. Divide that time by 10 to get the period of one revolution.

8. Repeat step 7 two more times, each time recording your results in your *Science Smart Journal.* Add the results of your three trials together, and then divide that time by 3 to get the average result.

9. Repeat steps 6 and 7 with a string 60 cm from the end of the straw to the eraser. And repeat steps 6 and 7 with a string of 90 cm.

10. In your *Science Smart Journal,* explain why you think you got the results you did. How does the experiment model the Solar System?

"So you see," Professor Jimenez said as he set the eraser down, "it's just like our Solar System. The farther a planet is from the Sun, the longer the period of its revolution."

"Not to sound disrespectful," Bob interrupted, "but we should probably push forward with your experiment. I worry that the McSweeneys will return with the police at any moment."

"Patience, child," the professor said. "The inner and outer planets aren't the only things out there in space. There are also comets, asteroids, and meteors. **Comets** are chunks of ice and dirt, actually. Comets have visible tails that can stretch for millions of kilometers. **Asteroids** are objects that revolve around the Sun that are too small to be considered full-fledged planets. Most asteroids revolve in a region called the **Asteroid Belt,** which is between the orbits of Mars and Jupiter. Some come close to Earth's orbit. About 65 million years ago one hit Earth near the Yucatán Peninsula in Mexico. The force of the impact kicked up dust and started fires, which may have caused the extinction of many, many species—dinosaurs included."

"So, I've heard," Bob sighed.

"Yes, yes, very sad," the professor nodded. "Last, there are chunks of rocks and dust in space called **meteoroids.** They're like asteroids, but smaller. When a meteoroid enters Earth's atmosphere, it's then called a **meteor.** If it hits Earth's surface, it's called a **meteorite.** Meteorites have fallen all over Earth, but most of them are so small, having mostly burnt up entering the atmosphere, that they're almost unnoticeable. It's truly amazing how much is up there," the professor added with a sigh. He stood there shaking his head, mumbling to himself, "Amazing, amazing."

"Earth to Professor," Bridget said, snapping her fingers. "Please hurry up. Bob's right. We don't have much time."

"Did you know that Earth is traveling 30 kilometers per second as it goes around the Sun? If I were traveling that fast," he said, snapping his fingers, "I'd be in New York City . . . *now*."

"That's fascinating, but . . . " Bridget began.

But then Angie interrupted, asking, "So why aren't we dizzy all the time if we're moving that fast?"

"Gravity," Barnaby cut in. "Earth has so much mass that it exerts a tremendous gravitational pull that holds us to the surface."

"Exactly," the professor agreed. "**Gravity** and **inertia** keep the planets in motion. Imagine that the planets are constantly falling away from the Sun; but for every inch they fall, they get pulled a certain amount back toward the Sun. The Sun has so much mass that it pulls everything toward it. It creates elliptical orbits, which are oval—rather than circular—orbits around the Sun. Observe," Professor Jimenez said as he handed Angie two push pins, a pencil, a rubber band, and a piece of cardboard.

TRY IT YOURSELF!

Eliciting Ellipses

MATERIALS
2 pieces of string of different lengths,
2 pushpins, paper, pencil, cardboard

STEPS
1. Tie each piece of string to create two loops—a smaller circle and a larger circle.
2. Stick two pushpins into the paper on top of your cardboard. Place the pushpins close enough that the smaller loop of string can rest loosely around them.
3. Using the tip of the pencil, pull the loop of string tight while keeping it on the pushpins. Keeping the tension constant, move the pencil around the pushpins drawing on the paper as you go.
4. Use the larger string loop and repeat step 3.
5. Record your observations in your *Science Smart Journal*, and think about how this models the orbits of the planets.

"So you see," the professor continued, "gravity is the force that pulls Earth—and all the planets—toward the Sun. And inertia, the tendency of a moving object to continue moving in the same direction or a stationary object to remain in place, is what keeps the planets moving forward."

Gravity and Inertia

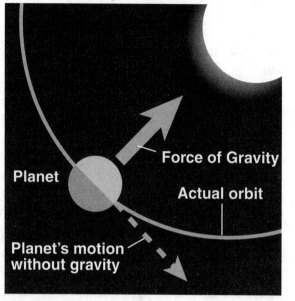

The professor continued his chatter, "The movement of one object around another, like Earth around the Sun, is called a **revolution.** A complete revolution of Earth around the Sun takes a year. But the amazing thing is that at the same time Earth is revolving around the Sun, it's also rotating around its own axis. The **axis** is an imaginary line passing through the north and south poles of a planet and through the planet's center. Earth's spinning on its axis, at a rate of about 1,600 kilometers per hour, is called its **rotation.** One rotation takes twenty-four hours, and it's this rotation that causes day and night. Angie, bring over my globe and the lamp from the corner."

TRY IT YOURSELF!

A Day in the Life

MATERIALS
1 globe, 1 lamp

STEPS
1. Take the lampshade off your lamp.
2. Place the globe about 1 meter away from your lamp.
3. Darken the room and turn on your lamp.
4. Find where you live on the globe. Turn the globe around once, noting when it's night and day. Record your observations in your *Science Smart Journal.*

"So when you're facing the Sun it's daytime, and when you're not," the professor added, "it's nighttime. Now, while Earth is revolving around the Sun and rotating around its axis, it's also tilted on its axis. The axis causes the seasons. Because Earth is tilted, some parts of the planet get more sunlight than others. See," he added, pulling a book out from behind him and flipping open to exactly the page he needed.

The Northern Hemisphere's Seasons

Professor Jimenez continued, "In January Earth is closest to the Sun, and in July it's farthest from the Sun. However, what determines the seasons is the tilt of the Earth. When a region of Earth is closer to the Sun because it is tilted toward the Sun, it's summer in that region. When that region tilts away from the Sun, it's winter.

"On two days each year, the noon Sun is overhead at exactly 23.5° south or 23.5° north. These two days are called the **summer solstice** and the **winter solstice.** In the northern hemisphere, where we live, the summer solstice is the longest day of the year and the winter solstice is the shortest. There are also two days a year when the length of the day is equal to the length of the night. When it happens in March, it's called the **vernal equinox.** When day and night are equal in September, it's called the **autumnal equinox.**"

"Well, all this has been real fascinating, Professor," Bridget interrupted, "but can we get to the big experiment? We'd kinda like to get a move on."

"Understood—but there's one last thing, if you can sit still for another moment," he said.

"Just one more thing?" Bridget asked.

"Promise, but it's a pretty amazing thing: eclipses. But first you have to understand a little bit about the phases of a moon," the professor added, stretching his legs and taking a sip of Babette's milk.

"You said one more," Bridget whined.

"It is just one more thing," he told her, "but you see, dear lady, this is science, and in science there is never just one thing. Everything is connected. Every idea leads to a hundred other ideas. So, yes, eclipses, but first you have to understand that as Earth revolves around the Sun so too does the Moon revolve around Earth—every 27.3 days. Now answer me this: When you get into bed at night and you turn off the lights, could you see a baseball sitting on your dresser?"

"If it were perfectly dark," Bridget said, thinking for a long moment, "no, I doubt it."

"Then how can you see the Moon?" Professor Jimenez asked, and for a moment the children were stumped. "Because it reflects the sunlight. Just because it's nighttime, it doesn't mean the Sun stops shining, right? And that's exactly why there are **phases,** or different shapes you can see from Earth, of the Moon. Each phase depends on how much of the sunlit side of the Moon is facing Earth. Now

eclipses—you thought I'd forgotten, didn't you?—happen when the Moon's shadow hits Earth or Earth's shadow hits the Moon. When the Moon passes between Earth and the Sun, a **solar eclipse** occurs. When Earth is directly between the Moon and the Sun during a full moon, a **lunar eclipse** occurs. See," he said, taking out his book again.

Lunar Eclipse

from space　　　　**from Earth**

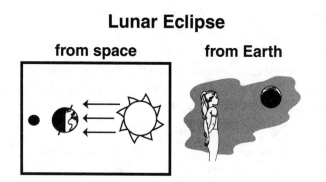

Solar Eclipse

from space　　　　**from Earth**

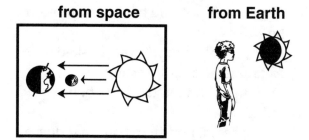

"Okay, now we're done, right? So what's your big experiment that you need help with?" Bridget asked almost breathlessly.

"We just finished it," Professor Jimenez laughed. "I wanted to see how long I could get five kids to sit still while I talked about the Sun-Earth-Moon System."

"Professor Jimenez," a weary voice came over a staticky sounding megaphone, "this is the police department. The paleontology department thinks you have a dinosaur in there *again*. Please do us all a favor and come talk to them."

"Again?" Bob asked.

"Oh yes, every couple of weeks Dr. McSweeney accuses me of harboring a different extinct animal. Last month, she swore I had a flock of dodo birds in my pantry."

"Did you?" Barnaby asked.

"How should I know?" he said, smiling. "I'm just a blind, old man. Now you better get a move on while I distract them. There's a secret passage behind the bookcase. It leads right back to your basement, Barnaby. You better get Bob back to the crack in the basement quick. It's not safe having a dinosaur flying around the streets."

"You knew all along?" Angie asked.

"Of course," he said, shrugging.

"But I do not understand," Babette cut in. "You are blind, no?"

"Yes," he said, nodding, "but that doesn't mean I can't see what's going on right in front of me. Now get a move on. Your parents said that you can reopen the crack just by opening the copy of *On the Origin of Species by Means of Natural Selection* on the shelf downstairs."

"Thank you, Professor," Angie said, jumping up on him to kiss his cheek.

"It was my pleasure. Come by any time. Next time you're here maybe we'll start in on the tides."

"Professor, please," the police officer on the megaphone called out, "Dr. McSweeney swears she saw a pterodactyl go in there. She won't leave me alone until you come out."

Professor Jimenez went to go answer the door, and Bob and the kids all ran over to the bookcase back in the corner. The bookcase opened before them, as if by magic, exposing a dark secret passageway.

"I guess this is it. Who first?" Babette volunteered, followed by Bob, and then Angie. Bridget and Barnaby were the last two left. They could hear the professor telling the police that there was nothing to see, and they both couldn't help but laugh.

Bridget heard the footsteps approaching quickly, and without thinking she shoved Barnaby into the secret entrance and followed a second later. The passageway was like a huge slide, and they landed right after another, one on top of another, in the laundry basket in the basement.

"Are you guys okay?" Angie asked.

"I think so," Barnaby said.

Just then from upstairs, Barnaby heard his parents yell, "Hello, we're home."

"Bob," Angie and Barnaby said simultaneously. "We've got to get you back."

"But what if I don't want to go," Bob said, kicking at the ground. "I kinda like it here. You have frozen burritos. We don't have them in the Mesozoic era." And while Bob complained that where he comes from baseball season wouldn't start for millions of years, Barnaby pulled down their copy of Darwin's classic book. He flipped it open, and the crack in the wall split wide again. "I mean, I am really going to miss you guys," Bob sighed.

"Here," Barnaby said, handing his friend the book, "if you have this you can reopen the crack anytime you want."

"Really?" Bob said, pressing the copy of *On the Origin of Species by Means of Natural Selection* to his chest using his wings. "You mean it?"

"Of course," Angie said, hugging their dinosaur friend, "we love you, silly."

"Well, I love you guys too," Bob said, with tears in his eyes as they all group-hugged. Even Beauregard, who'd been hiding in a warm spot back by the furnace, hopped out onto a nearby table to meow a goodbye.

"Angie! Barnaby!" their father screamed from the top of the basement steps, probably noticing the mess they'd left upstairs. "What is going on here?"

"That's my sign to go," Bob said as he put a wing through the crack. "I'll be back, though. I promise."

"We'll be here," Barnaby said as they all waved goodbye.

"What happened to the kitchen?" their mom yelled, presumably having noticed the wall Bob had busted through.

The kids could only cringe as they thought about the mess they'd made learning all they'd managed to learn that night. Somehow, though, they each knew that no matter how much trouble they were about to get into, it was all worth it. How many times do you get to ride on the back of a dinosaur? It was not the Friday night they had planned, but as Bridget, who was listening intently to her portable radio, yelled, "The Yankees won! The Yankees won!" they all knew they wouldn't trade all they'd learned this Friday night for anything in the world.

If you look at a candle flame, you'll notice that it's probably reddish near the wick but yellow near the top. If you look at a flame on a gas stove, you'll see it burns blue at its base. That's because stove flames burn much hotter than candle flames. For the same reason, stars come in a range of colors. The star Betelgeuse burns red, while the star Rigel burns bluish-white. That's because Betelgeuse burns at about 3,200° Celsius and Rigel burns about 12,700° Celsius. Using information about a star's color, scientists can estimate a star's temperature. Do the following experiment to see what can be revealed about the temperature of a glowing object by its color.

TRY IT YOURSELF!

Wish Upon a Star

MATERIALS
2 foot-long insulated wires, 2 weak C batteries, 1 flashlight bulb, 2 new C batteries, electrical tape

STEPS
1. To find 2 weak C batteries, remove C batteries from an old flashlight or portable radio. (The experiment won't ruin the batteries; you can replace them after you're done.)

— *continued on next page* —

— *continued from previous page* —

2. Take one end of an insulated wire and secure it with electrical tape to the negative end of one of the weak C batteries. Take another piece of insulated wire and secure it to the positive end of one of the weak C batteries with electrical tape.

3. Hold the free end of one of the wires to the bottom of the light bulb. Hold the other loose wire end against the metal side of the bulb. The light bulb should go on.

4. After a minute put the batteries, wires, and light bulb down and carefully touch the bulb to test the temperature. Record your observations in your *Science Smart Journal.*

5. Disconnect the wires. Tape the two weak C batteries together, connecting the positive end of the first battery to the negative end of the second battery.

6. Repeat steps 2–4 with the two weak C batteries connected.

7. Remove the wires. Repeat steps 2–4 with only one of the new C batteries.

8. Repeat steps 2–5 with both new C batteries.

9. Consider your observations and connect what you've just discovered with what you know about the temperature and colors of stars.

Matching

Match each word in the column below with its correct
meaning in the column on the next page.

1. Meteorite   _____
2. Phases   _____
3. Asteroid Belt   _____
4. Earth   _____
5. Revolution   _____
6. Outer planets   _____
7. Jupiter   _____
8. Summer solstice   _____
9. Uranus   _____
10. Equinox   _____
11. Rotation   _____
12. Comets   _____
13 Asteroids   _____
14. Venus   _____
15. Eclipse   _____
16. Meteors   _____
17. Inner planets   _____
18. Mars   _____
19. Earth's axis   _____
20. Pluto   _____
21. Saturn   _____
22. Winter solstice   _____
23. Neptune   _____
24. Mercury   _____
25. Meteoroids   _____

A. The area between the orbits of Mars and Jupiter where most asteroids in the Solar System are found

B. The small, frozen ninth planet from the Sun in our Solar System

C. The shortest day of the year, usually December 21 in the northern hemisphere

D. The spinning of an object around its axis

E. A meteoroid that has hit Earth's surface

F. The five planets in our Solar System farthest from the Sun: Jupiter, Saturn, Neptune, Uranus, and Pluto

G. The most massive planet in our Solar System

H. The sixth planet from the Sun in our Solar System and the only known planet that is less dense than water

I. The seventh planet from the Sun; it looks bluish because of traces of methane in its atmosphere

J. The planet that is thirty times farther from the Sun than is Earth

K. The closest planet to the Sun and the second smallest planet in our Solar System

L. An imaginary line passing through the north and south poles of a planet and through the planet's center

M. Objects revolving around the Sun that are too small to be considered full-fledged planets

N. Four relatively small planets with rocky surfaces that are closest to the Sun: Mercury, Venus, Earth, and Mars

O. Chunks of rocks and dust in space

P. Different shapes of the Moon that you can see from Earth

Q. The fourth planet from the Sun; it has two very small moons, Phobos and Deimos

R. An event that occurs when the Moon's shadow hits Earth or Earth's shadow hits the Moon, causing a total or partial blockage of sunlight

S. The movement of one object around another

T. Pieces of ice and dirt that orbit the Sun and have visible tails that can stretch for millions of kilometers long

U. The third planet from the Sun and the only planet that is seventy percent water

V. The longest day of the year, usually around June 21 in the northern hemisphere

W. Second planet from the Sun in our Solar System

X. When the length of the day is equal to the length of the night

Y. Meteoroids once they enter Earth's atmosphere

Chapter 12
Practice Test

Choose the best answer choice for the questions below. Some questions will test you on information you've already read, while others will require you to read charts, graphs, and tables. Write your answer choices in your *Science Smart Journal*. The Answer Key begins on page 253.

1. The acacia tree and ants have a cooperative relationship. The acacia tree produces nectar on its leaves. The ants eat nectar and other insects like caterpillars.

    Which explains the relationship between the acacia and the ant?

    A. The acacia is eaten by the ants, and the ants destroy the acacia.
    B. The ants decompose the acacia after it dies, and the acacia feeds the ants.
    C. The ants get energy from the acacia nectar and eat insects that might eat the acacia leaves.
    D. The acacia provides energy for the ants, and the ants carry water to the acacia leaves.

2. Plants need to have their seeds spread around. Look at the pictures of seeds below to help you answer the following question.

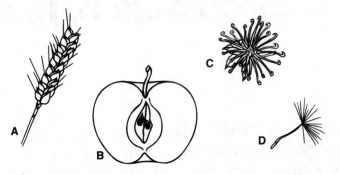

Which seed gets transported primarily by sticking to animals' fur coats?

A. A
B. B
C. C
D. D

3. A food chain shows how energy flows through an ecosystem. A food chain shows where each animal gets its energy. A fish might eat seaweed. Then a raccoon might eat a fish. Here is an example of the energy flow:

Seaweed ⟶ Fish ⟶ Raccoon

Food chains can be connected to make a food web. This picture is the food web for a field near a forest.

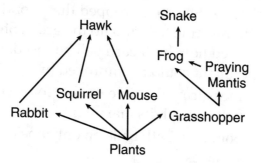

Which of these gives a food chain that can be found in the picture?

A. Plants ⟶ rabbit ⟶ squirrel ⟶ mouse

B. Mouse ⟶ hawk ⟶ rabbit ⟶ plants

C. Grasshopper ⟶ praying mantis ⟶ snake ⟶ frog

D. Plants ⟶ grasshopper ⟶ praying mantis ⟶ frog

4. Trina wanted to find out which of her rubber balls can bounce the highest. She took the first ball and dropped it onto the cement sidewalk. She then dropped the second ball from the same height onto the grass. She recorded how high each ball bounced. Her experiment could be improved by—

    A. measuring the time it takes for each ball to reach its maximum height
    B. bouncing both balls on only one of the surfaces
    C. dropping the second ball from a greater height
    D. bouncing the first ball on the cement two times

5. Evaporation is one step of the water cycle. Which of these provides the energy for evaporation?

    A. waves
    B. sunlight
    C. decomposers
    D. bacteria

6. Cows get an important nutrient from grass when they eat it. Cows then give this nutrient back to the ground in waste materials, or when they decompose after they die. This nutrient is important for all living things.

   What is this nutrient called?
   A. oxygen
   B. nitrogen
   C. carbon
   D. sodium

7. Which of the following is true about the summer solstice?
   A. The hours of daylight and night are equal.
   B. It has the longest hours of night in the year.
   C. The tides are the highest of the year.
   D. It has the longest hours of daylight in the year.

8. What is a valid conclusion from the information in the table and map below?

Station	Distance of station from earthquake epicenter
1	140 miles
2	30 miles
3	170 miles

A. Most earthquakes happen in California.

B. The epicenter was probably inside the borders of Nevada.

C. The epicenter was on the border between Oregon and California.

D. The earthquake happened closest to station 3.

9. Kevin was making cookies. He put two eggs into a mixing bowl. Then he added baking soda to the bowl. By accident, he added red wine vinegar to the bowl instead of oil.

Kevin noticed some changes after the vinegar was added. Which observation is a sign that a chemical change occurred in the mixing bowl?

   A. When the eggs were mixed, they turned light yellow.
   B. When Kevin added red wine vinegar to the baking soda, a lot of bubbles appeared.
   C. When the egg carton was opened, one of the eggs was broken.
   D. The baking soda got wet when it was added to the eggs.

10. Maya is going to perform an experiment during science class. She is going to shake a rock in a container of water. What could Maya do, before and after the experiment, to see if a physical change occurred?

   A. Use a ruler to measure the size of the rock.
   B. Take the temperature of the rock
   C. Look for sparks during the experiment.
   D. Draw a picture of the rock to see if it changes color.

11. Which choice is an example of kinetic energy changing into potential energy?
    A. A person climbs to the top of a slide.
    B. A television is turned on.
    C. A breeze moves a flag.
    D. A tree branch falls to the ground.

12. Amy is standing on her roller blades. In front of her is a large wooden ball.

P   Q

What will happen if Amy gives the ball a push?
    A. Amy will move toward P and the ball will move toward Q.
    B. Amy and the ball will move toward Q.
    C. Amy will move toward Q and the ball will move toward P.
    D. The ball will move toward Q and pull Amy toward Q.

13. Which of the techniques listed below is a way for farmers to prevent erosion of topsoil?
    A. adding fertilizer to their crops
    B. rotating their crops
    C. planting strips of grass between crops
    D. cutting down trees around the fields

14. An energy pyramid shows how much energy is available along the steps of a food chain. It illustrates the way that energy moves around in an ecosystem.

    In a pond, a food chain is made up of seaweed, small fish, large fish, and eagles. Which picture below shows the correct energy pyramid for this food chain?

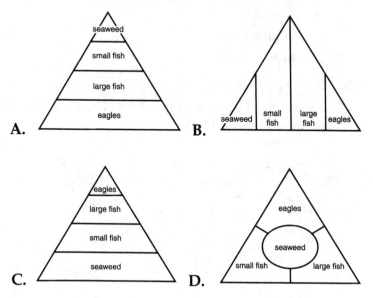

15. Farmers use sprinklers to irrigate their crops.

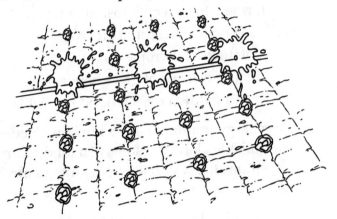

Which function of the water cycle is most like what is shown in the picture?

A. condensation

B. runoff

C. evaporation

D. precipitation

16. A box of pencils falls off a table in Janice's room when she slams the door. The path of the box is shown below.

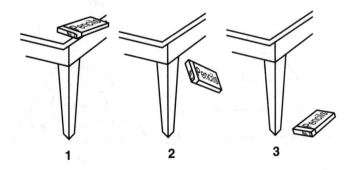

1   2   3

What type of energy conversion is happening between pictures 1 and 2?

A. Kinetic energy is being converted into chemical energy.

B. Potential energy is being converted into chemical energy.

C. Kinetic energy is being converted into potential energy.

D. Potential energy is being converted into kinetic energy.

17. The flow chart below shows the percent of energy used in the United States that comes from different energy sources. Use this chart to help you answer the next two questions.

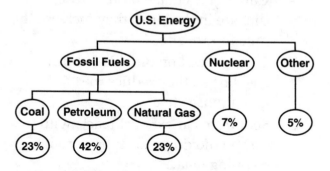

According to the chart, how much of the energy used in the United States comes from hydroelectric power?

A. 0–5%

B. 7%

C. 23%

D. 42%

18. Which of the following energy sources would most likely be found in an average U.S. home?

    A. solar energy
    B. nuclear energy
    C. coal
    D. petroleum

19. Carbon dioxide in the atmosphere traps heat coming up from the earth. It keeps the heat from escaping into space. This is called the greenhouse effect.

    When cars burn gasoline, how does that affect the greenhouse effect process?

    A. Car engines make more carbon dioxide in the air so they increase the greenhouse effect.
    B. Cars use carbon dioxide to burn gasoline so they reduce the greenhouse effect.
    C. Soot from car exhaust reacts with carbon dioxide and stops it from trapping heat.
    D. Heat from car engines destroys carbon dioxide reducing the greenhouse effect.

20. Which layer of Earth's atmosphere is most suitable for jet travel?
    A. stratosphere
    B. mesosphere
    C. troposphere
    D. ionosphere

21. The atmosphere exerts pressure on Earth's surface because it?
    A. holds heat
    B. has weight
    C. holds moisture
    D. obtains energy from the Sun

Answer Key

CHAPTER 1: INTRODUCTION

Sugar and Salt
<u>Results:</u> The sugar and salt should disappear. The rice shouldn't disappear. Some substances are soluble, such as sugar and salt, and some aren't, such as rice.

CHAPTER 2: THE PROPERTIES OF MATTER

The Phases of Matter
<u>Results:</u> The perfume should seem to disappear and leave a detectable odor. The water should take the shape of the cup it's poured into. The marble will stay the same shape, regardless of whether it is in the bowl or the cup. This experiment highlights the physical properties of each of these substances. Solids have definite shape, liquids have definite volume but an indefinite shape, and gases have no definite volume or shape.

Temperature, Gases, and Liquids

<u>Results:</u> The gas in the soda causes the inflation of the balloon. The more gas there is, the bigger the balloon should become. Warmer liquids can't hold as much gas in them, so the warmer soda lets more gas escape into the balloon. The cold soda holds more gas in it, so less comes out into the balloon. Therefore the balloon over the warm soda should become more inflated.

The Density Test

<u>Results:</u> It's difficult to tell, just by looking at something, whether it will float on water or not. Some small objects—the sugar cube and the chocolate cube—sink when they are put into a bowl of water. This means they are denser than water. The butter, on the hand, whether it is a stick or a cube, floats. This means that the butter is less dense than water.

Mixing Up the Medicine

<u>Results:</u> The baking soda and vinegar, when mixed, create bubbles that appear in the solution. We know that a chemical change has taken place because the formation of bubbles are a clear indication that a chemical process is occurring. (Since heat isn't added to this experiment, we know it's not a simple physical change from liquid to gas.)

Gunk

<u>Results:</u> This is another example of a chemical change. The starch and glue don't just mix—like adding salt into a glass of water—they undergo a

chemical reaction. The gunk is a new substance with different properties than what it was formed from.

The Unbalanced Bubble Meter
Results: Force is created when something experiences a push or pull. The unbalanced bubble meter is a way to measure the amount of force being applied to the bottle. When it is stationary, the bubble should rest at zero. The harder you push or pull the bottle, the farther the bubble should move.

✍ QUIZ #1 ✍

1. D
2. B
3. B
4. A
5. B

✍ QUIZ #2 ✍

Matching

1. I
2. H
3. E
4. F
5. A
6. C
7. G
8. B
9. D

Chapter 3: Motions and Forces

Describing Motion
1. 60 feet south
2. Southwest
3. Second base

A Penny Saved
Results: The penny will probably fall into the cup. This is because the inertia of the penny is greater than the force of friction between the penny and the paper. Try the same experiment using sandpaper instead of notebook paper, and you should see that the penny is pulled off along with the sandpaper. That's because sandpaper produces more friction than notebook paper—enough to overcome the penny's inertia.

Faster Friction
Results: The marble will roll the farthest over the surface with the least friction. In this case, the marble should have rolled the farthest distance over the aluminum foil and the shortest distance over the hand towel. (Results may vary based on things like the thickness of your hand towels and the "stickiness" of your plastic wrap.)

The Pull of Gravity
Results: You should note that the paper clip always hangs straight down no matter what direction you tilt the ruler. This is because gravity is a force that pulls

straight down toward Earth. For the same reason, when you drop a ball, it always falls straight to the ground.

The Distance Race

<u>Results:</u> The heavier can should travel farther. When you release either can, potential energy begins changing into kinetic energy. The heavier can has more potential at the top of the ramp, and therefore it has more kinetic energy at the bottom of the ramp. Because the heavier can has more energy, it will roll farther before that energy runs out because of friction.

✍ QUIZ #3 ✎

One possible experiment:
Experiment Title: Magnetic Pull
Materials: string, tape, metal washer, ruler, 2 identical magnets
Steps:
1. Tie the metal washer to the string and tape the string to a table so that the washer is about three or four inches from the ground.
2. Tape one magnet to each end of the ruler.
3. Put the ruler beneath the washer, so that the washer hangs above the middle. Note what measurement is at the middle.
4. Slide the ruler so that one end moves closer to the washer. Stop at the point that the washer moves toward the magnet. Note in your *Science Smart Journal* how far that point is from the center of the ruler.

5. Recenter and repeat step 4 five times. Determine the average of the distances from the center when the magnet started to move.
6. Repeat steps 4 and 5, moving the ruler in the other direction.

Before you do your experiment, what is your prediction for the results?

You should have predicted that while the washer hangs directly between the two magnets the forces are balanced. The point at which the forces become unbalanced is the point at which the washer moves.

What results did you get?

If your magnets were of equal strengths, your measurements were accurate, and you moved the ruler carefully, you should have noted that the points at which the forces became unbalanced were at approximately equal distances from the center of the ruler.

If your results are different from what you predicted, explain why.

Your magnets may not have been equal or strong enough. You may have moved the ruler too quickly to get accurate results. Your washer may not be a metal that has magnetic properties. You may have averaged your results incorrectly.

✍ QUIZ #4 ✍

Matching

1. C
2. J
3. F
4. K
5. I
6. B
7. H
8. E
9. G
10. A
11. D
12. L

CHAPTER 4: ENERGY

Catch!

<u>Results:</u> The higher the sock is raised above your helper's hand the more potential energy it has. The farther it falls the more of that potential energy will have been converted into kinetic energy. It will feel like it fell harder because it has more momentum based on its faster speed.

Hidden Potential

<u>Results:</u> The energy to drive the stake into the soil comes from the conversion of potential energy (the ball held above the stake) into kinetic energy (the ball falling to the ground, accelerating due to gravity). The higher you hold the ball and the more the ball

weighs, the farther it will knock the stake into
the soil.

The Conservation of Dizziness

<u>Results:</u> The lid should spin in the opposite direction
of the way you rotate it. The spinning should cause
the string to wind in the opposite direction. When the
lid stops spinning in the original direction, it will
reverse and spin the opposite way. This will continue
until the string is completely unwound. Why? The
law of conservation of energy states that energy
cannot be created or destroyed. So when you add
energy to wind the string, the energy has to go
somewhere. In effect, it's stored in the wound string,
which releases the energy when you release the lid.
The lid keeps spinning until friction causes the
system to lose energy.

Hot, Hot, Hot

<u>Results:</u> Certain substances conduct heat better than
others. The utensil that conducts heat the best will
melt the butter the fastest—and will drop the button
the fastest. The button on the metal fork should fall
first, followed by the plastic fork, and then the
wooden spoon.

Spin, Spin, Spin

<u>Results:</u> The circle should start spinning shortly after
the light is turned on. This is because as the lightbulb
heats up it heats the air around it. Hot air is less
dense then cold air, so the hot air rises thereby
creating a convection current. This convection current
is what causes the circle to spin.

It's a Refract, Jack

<u>Results:</u> Light travels at different speeds through different substances, and light only travels in straight lines. So when light passes from air to water, as it does in this case, it slows down. This slowing down causes the angle at which the light is traveling to change, which is why it looks like the pencil is bending at the point the pencil enters the water.

✍ QUIZ #5 ✍

One possible experiment:
Experiment Title: Am I Opaque?
Materials: Flashlight, white cardboard, clay, any objects you want to test (suggestions: cellophane, different plastic containers, hand towel, aluminum foil, book, paper, mirror, etc.)
Steps:
1. Stand the cardboard upright in the clay.
2. Select one object and hold it front of the white cardboard.
3. Aim the flashlight at the object and the cardboard.
4. Note what you see on the white cardboard in your *Science Smart Journal*.
5. Sort the objects into groups depending on whether they are opaque, translucent, or transparent.

Before you do your experiment, what is your prediction for the results?
Cellophane will be transparent; plastic containers may be opaque, translucent, or transparent; towels, aluminum foil, paper, mirror, book will be opaque.

What results did you get?
Results will depend on what items you choose to test. Most items will likely be opaque.
If your results are different from what you predicted, explain why.
You may come across some items that look opaque but end up actually being translucent. This is because under bright, direct light enough light is able to slip through to be noticeable on the cardboard.

✍ QUIZ #6 ✍

1. C
2. A
3. B
4. D

✍ QUIZ #7 ✍
Matching

1. A
2. B
3. J
4. G
5. D
6. C
7. N

8. M
9. H
10. F
11. E
12. K
13. L
14. I

CHAPTER 5: LIVING SYSTEMS

A Yeasty Mess

Results: On the slide with the warm-water mixture, you should see the yeast feeding on the sugar. The yeast may be bubbling as it produces carbon dioxide. On the slide with a cold-water mixture, you should see inactive yeast cells.

Cells

Results:

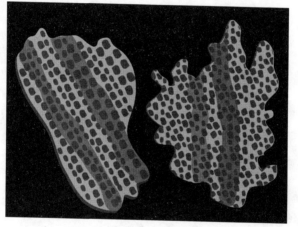

Cork Cell

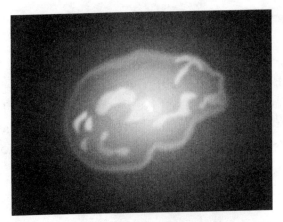

Cheek cells

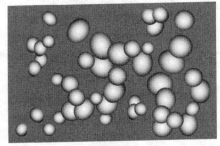

Yeast

Quick Calculations: Surface Area

<u>Results:</u>

Cube A Volume: 1

Cube B Surface Area: 150

Cube C Surface-to-Volume Ratio: 5

Tea for Two

Results: You should note that the first color changes in the water occur near the tea bag. The more the tea bag is dipped in the hot water, the darker the water will turn. This is because of diffusion. The tea diffuses through the tea bag and spreads out into the water.

They're Good for Your Heart

Results: Essentially, the beans use the water to respire and change food energy into other forms of energy. Thermal energy is one form of energy that is released through the beans' respiration process. Beans can't respire without water. Therefore, the temperature in the jar with the soaked beans should be higher than in the jar of dry beans.

✍ QUIZ #8 ✍

Growing up, uP, UP

Results: You should see the corn seedlings start to sprout roots. Water was necessary for the growth, and so is oxygen. If you calculated your average growth accurately, you should be able to estimate the amount of growth for any given amount of time. (The corn seedlings should grow at a constant rate, if the water, oxygen, and sunlight are kept constant.) Seedlings most likely did not grow if they were given too much or too little water. A seedling also may have been left in a place where the temperature was either too hot or too cold.

1.	O	11.	E
2.	B	12.	M
3.	I	13.	N
4.	A	14.	J
5.	F	15.	R
6.	D	16.	L
7.	K	17.	G
8.	C	18.	Q
9.	P	19.	H
10.	S		

CHAPTER 6: REPRODUCTION AND HEREDITY

Eggs!

Results: The shell protects the developing chick. The yolk is food for the developing chick. The "white" inside of the egg protects the developing chick. The shell membrane allows gases to transfer into and out from the developing chick.

Meiosis

<u>Results:</u> This experiment demonstrates how meiosis works. One body cell begins with three shapes. Each shape duplicates and then divides and then divides again, forming four sex cells with one of each shape inside. In real life, body cells contain one set of chromosomes from each parent. These real body cells divide repeatedly to create offspring in much the same way that the shapes in this experiment did.

Traits

<u>Results:</u> You've just created a table of selected traits. These traits are each either dominant or recessive. (Read through the rest of the chapter for more information about the distinction.) Take a quick survey of which of these traits your friends exhibit. Whichever traits people most frequently have is probably the dominant trait for that pair of traits. The larger the sample of people, the more accurate your conclusions will be.

Making Mr. or Ms. Right

<u>Results:</u> There are no right answers for this game. However, you should note that dominant traits are expressed far more often than recessive traits.

✍ QUIZ #10 ✍

Punnett Square

1.
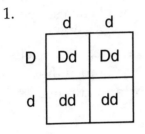

2. A

✍ QUIZ #11 ✍
Matching

1. M	11. K
2. N	12. R
3. C	13. O
4. P	14. A
5. Q	15. L
6. T	16. B
7. S	17. D
8. E	18. F
9. I	19. H
10. J	20. G

CHAPTER 7: ECOSYSTEMS

Investigate Your Own Ecosystem

<u>Results:</u> You should have been able to identify several different populations of animals and plants. Also you should note the nonliving aspect of your environment—for example, whether it is rocky, sunny, wet, shady, etc.

Connect the Web

<u>Results:</u>

It's Not Easy Being Green

Results: You should notice that a green area appears on the paper above where the leaves were. The green color is from the chlorophyll in the leaves, which is the green pigment that absorbs light needed for photosynthesis.

✍ QUIZ #12 ✍

In the Desert

Results: Your sponge will be lighter at the end of the 24 hours than at the beginning. Protecting your sponge from the sunlight is the best way to keep water from evaporating. Putting it in an airtight container is one effective strategy. Consider running the experiment again with two or three sponges. Store each in a different way and try to predict which will lose the least water.

✍ QUIZ #13 ✍
Matching

1. C
2. I
3. H
4. F
5. K
6. D
7. M

8. J
9. A
10. G
11. E
12. B
13. L

CHAPTER 8: ADAPTATION, EVOLUTION, AND DIVERSITY

Fossils
Results: You should have created two "fossils." One is a cast, a replica of the stick. The other is a mold in the shape of the shell.

Natural Selection
Results: Your partner should be able to pick more marshmallows off the blue paper than off the white paper. This is because marshmallows are more visible on the blue paper than on the white paper. For the same reason, animals that are camouflaged to match their environment often have a better chance at survival than animals that stand out.

All Thumbs
Results: It should seem easier to pick up the quarter when you are able to use your thumb. Having a thumb makes gripping possible, and animals that don't have thumbs must hold food and tools with two hands. They often don't have sophisticated skills for manipulating objects.

✍ QUIZ #14 ✍
Cactus finch: The most noticeable trait of the cactus finch is its beak, which has adapted especially for opening hard seeds.

Snowshoe hare: The snowshoe hare has large feet that enable it to run quickly on slick or shifting surfaces like ice or snow. The snowshoe hare is also white in the winter and reddish-brown in the summer to better blend in with its environment to avoid predators.

Desert cactus: Desert cacti have needlelike thorns to protect them from being eaten by desert creatures. They also have folds that swell, which allow these plants to hold water when rainfall is scarce.

Orangutan: Like humans, the orangutan has opposable thumbs. This trait allows these animals to climb and hang from trees and to fashion primitive tools. Their rusty coloring also helps them to blend in with their surroundings.

✍ QUIZ #15 ✍
Matching

1. F
2. E
3. C
4. D
5. A
6. B

Matching: Review

1. F
2. C
3. D
4. A
5. B
6. E

CHAPTER 9: THE GEOSPHERE

The Geosphere

Results: Your drawing represents the three basic layers of Earth. The blue outer edge is the crust, the red outer ring is the mantle, and the yellow inner circle is the core.

Tectonics

Results: As the water heats up you should notice that the sponges begin to float apart. This is because the water at the bottom of the pan floats upward. This models the basic theory of plate tectonics. Because plates of the lithosphere float on the asthenosphere (which is a soft layer of the mantle), when convection currents rise up, they cause Earth's plates to move.

Stress

Results: When you let go of the tongue depressor after bending it the first time, you'll notice that it doesn't return to its original shape but, rather, it stays bent to some degree. When you bend the tongue depressor until both ends touch, you'll notice that the tongue depressor starts to splinter and break at the point of the bend. Similar things happen when Earth's plates move. Stress on rocks causes them to change shape and to bend or break.

Erosion

<u>Results:</u> When the water flows over the mud balls, the mud will drain into the pan below. This is similar to when materials on Earth's crust break down due to weathering.

✍ QUIZ #16 ✍

Make Your Own Volcano

<u>Results:</u> The red water should rise up and out of the bottle. The red water will touch the underside of the sponge. This is a very basic model to show how magma can flow out of an ocean floor volcano and form underground volcanic mountains. It is a good model for hot spot volcanoes.

✍ QUIZ #17 ✍
Matching

1. F
2. H
3. C
4. P
5. N
6. E
7. G
8. D
9. I
10. J
11. B

12. R
13. K
14. T
15. S
16. M
17. Q
18. U
19. L
20. O
21. A

CHAPTER 10: THE HYDROSPHERE AND ATMOSPHERE

There's Air Up There

<u>Results:</u> You should notice that the clay ball at the bottom is the most "squished." This is because it had the most weight on it. In the same way, the greatest air pressure is closest to the ground, because, like the clay, it has the most layers weighing on top of it.

Clouds

<u>Results:</u> You'll note that a cloud forms as the moist air cools down. The cloud will form toward the top of the bottle, near the ice cube. It will slowly descend lower as the temperature equals out.

It's So Humid

<u>Results:</u> Water condenses on the outside of the container at the dew point. The water came from the air outside the container. Cool air can hold less water than warm air, so when the air around the container cooled to a certain point, the air couldn't hold the water any more and water condensed on the outside of the can.

The Greenhouse Effect

<u>Results:</u> The temperature in the plastic wrap covered bowl should have increased more quickly than in the uncovered bowl. This is because the gases around the soil absorb heat. In the uncovered bowl, those gases are free to circulate into the air. In the covered bowl, the gases are trapped. In much the same way, our atmosphere traps heat close to Earth.

Fronting

<u>Results:</u> The trick to doing this experiment successfully is to find a divider that doesn't let water seep in until it's removed. The red (warm) water should float to the top and the blue (cold) water should drop to the bottom. This models how a warm weather front meets a cold weather front. Cold air is denser so it naturally sinks to the bottom.

✍ QUIZ #18 ✍

Reading a Weather Map

1. A
2. C
3. Results will vary—even the best weatherperson isn't always right—but after a week of tracking how fronts are moving, you should be able to make generally accurate predictions.

✍ QUIZ #19 ✍
Matching

1. L
2. I
3. H
4. M
5. E
6. A
7. K
8. B
9. O
10. D
11. J
12. C
13. G
14. N
15. F
16. P

CHAPTER 11:
EARTH AND THE SOLAR SYSTEM

Around and Around

Results: You should note that the longer the string is, the longer it takes to complete a revolution around you. The same is true in the solar system. The farther a planet is from the Sun, the longer it takes to complete a revolution.

Eliciting Ellipses

Results: You should note that both loops of string help create ellipses around the pushpins. The larger loop of string creates a larger ellipse, while the smaller loop of string creates a smaller ellipse. This roughly models or the inner and outer planets of our Solar System as they travel in revolutions around the Sun.

A Day in the Life

<u>Results:</u> When a region of Earth faces the Sun, it's daytime in that region. This experiment should help you see that the rotation of Earth is what causes day and night.

✍ QUIZ #20 ✍

Wish Upon a Star

<u>Results:</u> You should note that the new batteries make the light a different color and brightness than old batteries do. The same is true when you connect two batteries instead of one. In the same way, stars will be a different color and brightness depending on their temperature. The strength of the batteries is a way of increasing the temperature of the bulb.

✍ QUIZ #21 ✍
Matching

1. E
2. P
3. A
4. U
5. S
6. F
7. G
8. V
9. I
10. X
11. D
12. T
13. M
14. W
15. R
16. Y
17. N
18. Q
19. L
20. B
21. H
22. C
23. J
24. K
25. O

CHAPTER 12: PRACTICE TEST

1. C
2. C
3. D
4. B
5. B
6. B
7. D
8. B
9. B
10. A
11. A
12. A
13. C
14. C
15. D
16. D
17. A
18. D
19. A
20. A
21. B

Glossary

acceleration: a change in either the velocity or the direction of travel of an object (Ch. 3)

adaptation: a characteristic that helps an organism survive and reproduce in its environment (Ch. 8)

air density: the mass of a given volume of air (Ch. 10)

air masses: bodies of air that have properties determined by the part of Earth's surface over which they develop (Ch. 10)

asexual reproduction: the reproductive process that does not involve the union of gametes from two different individuals, e.g., cell division or budding (Ch. 6)

Asteroid Belt: the area between the orbits of Mars and Jupiter where most asteroids in the solar system are found (Ch. 11)

asteroids: objects that revolve around the Sun that are too small to be considered full-fledged planets (Ch. 11)

atmosphere: the layer of gases that surrounds Earth (Ch. 9 and 10)

autumnal equinox: the day in autumn in which the length of the day is equal to the length of the night (Ch. 11)

axis: an imaginary line passing through the north and south poles of a planet and through the planet's center (Ch. 11)

balanced forces: equal forces that act on an object and cancel each other out (Ch. 3)

biosphere: living organisms and their environment (Ch. 9)

body cells: cells that have been specialized to do certain jobs, e.g., blood and skin cells (Ch. 6)

boiling point: the temperature at which a substance changes from a liquid to a gas (Ch. 2)

cell: the basic unit of all living things (Ch. 5)

cell membrane: the semipermeable structure that covers the outside of the cell (Ch. 5)

cell wall: a rigid structure that supports and protects plant cells (Ch. 5)

chemical change: a change that occurs when a substance changes into a different substance with new characteristics (Ch. 2)

chlorophyll: the main pigment that is involved in photosynthesis (Ch. 7)

chloroplast: part of a cell that converts light energy into chemical energy (Ch. 5)

chromosome: the structure in a cell that contains instructions that "tell" a cell how to develop (Ch. 5 and 6)

comets: pieces of ice and dirt that orbit the Sun and have visible tails that can stretch for millions of kilometers (Ch. 11)

community: a population of different animals living and interacting in a specific location (Ch. 7)

complex organism: a many-celled organism, such as an animal (Ch. 5)

compression: stress that squeezes rock until it breaks (Ch. 9)

condensation: occurs when a substance changes from a gas to a liquid (Ch. 10)

conduction: the process in which heat moves through a material or from one material to another (Ch. 4)

consumer: an animal that eats other animals or plants (Ch. 7)

convection: a heat transfer by the motion of a heat-carrying medium (Ch. 4, 8, and 9)

core: the dense center of Earth (Ch. 9)

crust: the thin outer surface of Earth (Ch. 9)

cytoplasm: the liquid part of the cell in which most of the cell's life processes occur (Ch. 5)

Darwin, Charles: the scientist who developed the theory of natural selection in the early 1800s after studying animals on the Galápagos Islands; he wrote *On the Origin of Species by Means of Natural Selection* (Ch. 8)

decomposer: anything that breaks down dead organisms, returning their energy to the soil (Ch. 7)

density: the amount of mass an object has compared to its volume (Ch. 2)

dew point: the temperature at which condensation happens (Ch. 10)

diffuse reflection: when light bounces in many different directions (Ch. 4)

diffusion: the movement of molecules from an area of high concentration to one of low concentration (Ch. 5)

dominant trait: a characteristic of a living thing that will always express itself if it is contained in an organisms genes (Ch. 6)

Earth: the third planet from the Sun and the only planet that is seventy percent water (Ch. 11)

earthquake: the shaking and trembling that can result from the movement of rock beneath Earth's surface (Ch. 9)

eclipse: an event that occurs when the Moon's shadow hits Earth or Earth's shadow hits the Moon, causing a total or partial blockage of sunlight (Ch. 11)

ecosystem: a community of organisms interacting with each other and with the nonliving environment (Ch. 7)

eggs: female sex cells (Ch. 6)

element: a substance that cannot be broken down into simpler substances (Ch. 2)

energy: the ability to do work or produce change (Ch. 4)

erosion: the movement of rocks or rock particles by wind, water, ice, or gravity (Ch. 9)

evaporation: the process by which water absorbs enough energy from the Sun to turn from a liquid to a gaseous state (Ch. 10)

external fertilization: the reproduction process in which the female releases eggs into water, and the male's sperm swim to the eggs and fertilize them (Ch. 6)

extinct: when an organism doesn't exist anymore (Ch. 8)

fault: a break in the lithosphere at which slabs of crust slip past each other (Ch. 9)

fertilization: occurs when sperm from a male unite with eggs from a female (Ch. 6)

food chain: a model that demonstrates how energy is passed from organism to organism in an ecosystem (Ch. 7)

food web: a combination of food chains in an ecological community (Ch. 7)

force: a push or pull exerted on matter (Ch. 3)

friction: a force that resists motion between two objects that are in contact (Ch. 3)

front: the area at which two air masses collide (Ch. 10)

gas: state of matter that has no definite shape or volume (Ch. 2)

gene: a section of a chromosome that controls a trait in an organism (Ch. 6)

genotype: the genetic makeup of an organism (Ch. 6)

geosphere: contains the lithosphere, hydrosphere, and atmosphere (rock and soil, water, and air) (Ch. 9)

gravity: the physical force that pulls all objects of mass together (Ch. 3 and 11)

greenhouse effect: the process by which gases in the atmosphere trap solar radiation and keep it near a planet's surface (Ch. 10)

habitat: a particular place in which an organism lives (Ch. 7)

heat: thermal energy that is transferred from something of higher temperature to something of lower temperature (Ch. 4)

heredity: the passing of traits from one generation to the next (Ch. 6)

humidity: the amount of water vapor in the air (Ch. 10)

hydrosphere: all the water masses that cover Earth (Ch. 9)

inertia: the tendency of an object to resist changes in motion (Ch. 3 and 11)

inner planets: the four relatively small planets, with rocky surfaces that are closest to the Sun: Mercury, Venus, Earth, and Mars (Ch. 11)

internal fertilization: the process by which sperm unite with eggs inside the female body (Ch. 6)

joule: a unit of energy or work (Ch. 4)

Jupiter: the most massive planet in our Solar System (Ch. 11)

kinetic energy: the energy of motion (Ch. 4)

lava: a molten mixture of rock, gas, and water vapor that has reached Earth's surface (Ch. 9)

law of conservation of energy: energy cannot be created or destroyed (Ch. 4)

liquid: matter that has a definite volume but an indefinite shape (Ch. 2)

lithosphere: the outer part of Earth's crust and mantle (Ch. 9)

lunar eclipse: an event that occurs when Earth is directly between the Moon and the Sun (Ch. 11)

magma: a molten mixture of rock, gas, and water vapor that makes up part of Earth's mantle (Ch. 9)

mantle: the hot, yet solid, layer between Earth's core and crust (Ch. 9)

Mars: the fourth planet from the Sun; it has two very small moons, Phobos and Deimos (Ch. 11)

mass: the amount of matter in an object (Ch. 2)

meiosis: the process by which sex cells are created (Ch. 6)

melting point: the temperature at which a substance changes from a solid to a liquid (Ch. 2)

Mendel, Gregor: an Austrian monk who did a series of experiments to show that traits in plants do not occur purely randomly (Ch. 6 and 8)

Mercury: the closest planet to the Sun and the second smallest planet in the Solar System (Ch. 11)

mesosphere: the atmospheric layer from which some radio waves are transmitted (Ch. 10)

meteor: a meteoroid once it enters Earth's atmosphere (Ch. 11)

meteorite: a meteoroid that has hit Earth's surface (Ch. 11)

meteoroids: chunks of rocks and dust in space (Ch. 11)

mitochondrion: the part of a cell that transforms energy in food molecules into energy needed by cells (Ch. 5)

mitosis: the process in which cells split into two new cells, each with the same type and number of chromosomes (Ch. 5)

mixture: a combination of two or more substances in which the basic identities of the original substances is not changed (Ch. 1)

molecule: the smallest particle a compound can be broken into without changing its identity (Ch. 5)

motion: the change in position of an object (Ch. 3)

natural selection: the natural process through which living things that are better adapted to their environments are more likely to survive and reproduce (Ch. 8)

Neptune: the planet that is thirty times farther from the Sun than is Earth (Ch.11)

Newton's first law of motion: bodies in motion remain in motion and bodies at rest remain at rest unless acted on by an outside force (Ch. 3)

Newton's second law of motion: the force acting on an object is equal to the mass of the object times the acceleration of the object (Ch. 3)

newton: a unit of force (Ch. 4)

niche: an animal's role in its environment (Ch. 7)

nitrogen cycle: a series of processes by which nitrogen passes from the air to the soil to organisms and back (Ch. 7)

nucleus: the part of the cell that controls all its activities (Ch. 5)

opaque: an object that blocks the passage of light (Ch. 4)

organ: a part of an animal or plant in which tissues work together to do a particular job (Ch. 5)

organism: the highest level of cellular organization; something that is alive (Ch. 5)

organ system: organs that work together to perform a life function (Ch. 5)

osmosis: diffusion of water through a cell membrane depending on the concentration of solutes on either side (Ch. 5 and 8)

outer planets: the five planets farthest from the Sun: Jupiter, Saturn, Neptune, Uranus, and Pluto (Ch. 11)

oxygen–carbon dioxide cycle: the cycle in which plants use carbon dioxide and release oxygen, and then animals use oxygen and release carbon dioxide (Ch. 7)

phases: the different shapes of the Moon that one can see from Earth (Ch. 11)

phenotype: the way genetic traits are expressed (Ch. 6)

photosynthesis: the process by which plants change sunlight into energy (Ch. 7 and 8)

physical change: when the physical properties of a substance change, but the identity of the substance does not (Ch. 2)

pigments: molecules that absorb light energy (Ch. 7)

plates: separate sections of Earth's lithosphere (Ch. 9)

Pluto: the small, frozen ninth planet in our Solar System (Ch. 11)

population: a particular species that lives in a particular place during a particular time (Ch. 7)

position: where an object is in relation to a reference point (Ch. 3)

potential energy: stored energy (Ch. 4)

precipitation: water that falls to Earth as hail, sleet, snow, or rain (Ch. 10)

producer: an organism that makes its own food (Ch. 7)

radiation: the process through which energy travels across a space in the form of waves or particles (Ch. 4)

recessive trait: a characteristic of a living thing that is not expressed in the presence of a dominant trait (Ch. 6)

refraction: the process in which light bends when it passes from one substance to another (Ch. 4)

regular reflection: occurs when light bounces directly back at its original source (Ch. 4)

reproduction: the process by which organisms produce young (Ch. 6)

respiration: a chemical process in which glucose molecules are broken down to release energy used by cells (Ch. 5)

revolution: the movement of one object around another (Ch. 11)

rotation: the spinning of an object around its axis (Ch. 11)

saturated: the state at which something cannot hold any more of a material in it (Ch. 10)

Saturn: the sixth planet from the Sun in our Solar System and the only known planet that is less dense than water (Ch. 11)

sediment: any small, solid particles from rocks or organisms that are moved by water, wind, or glaciers (Ch. 9)

selectively permeable: the ability of a membrane to allow some substances to enter the cell while keeping others out (Ch. 5)

sex cells: the specialized cells that some organisms use to produce offspring (Ch. 6)

sexual reproduction: the process in which the sperm from a male unites with one or more eggs from a female (Ch. 6)

shearing: stress that pushes a rock in opposite directions (Ch. 9)

simple organism: non-complex organism, such as bacteria (Ch. 5)

sister chromatids: the result when original chromosomes double, forming identical copies of themselves (Ch. 6)

solar eclipse: an event when the moon passes between Earth and the sun (Ch. 11)

solid: matter that has a definite shape and definite volume (Ch. 2)

solubility: the amount of a substance that can dissolve in 100 g of solvent at a given temperature (Ch. 2 and 8)

sperm: male sex cells (Ch. 6)

stratosphere: the atmospheric layer in which the ozone layer lies (Ch. 10)

stress: a force that can cause rock to change shape or volume (Ch. 9)

summer solstice: the longest day of the year, usually around June 21 in the northern hemisphere (Ch. 11)

tension: stress that pulls on a rock, stretching it enough to pull it apart (Ch. 9)

thermal equilibrium: a state of balance that occurs when two objects come in contact and the temperature of one becomes the same as the temperature of the other (Ch. 4)

thermosphere: the atmospheric layer extending from eighty to over five hundred kilometers in altitude (Ch. 10)

tissues: groups of cells working together to perform a function (Ch. 5)

traits: the unique characteristics of a living thing that were inherited (Ch. 6)

translucent: an object that lets some light through (Ch. 4)

transparent: an object that lets all light through (Ch. 4)

troposphere: the atmospheric layer in which clouds form and weather occurs (Ch. 10)

unbalanced forces: forces acting on an object unequally in some directions (Ch. 3 and 8)

Uranus: the seventh planet from the Sun; it looks bluish because of traces of methane in its atmosphere (Ch. 11)

vacuole: the part of the cell in which water, food, and other materials are stored (Ch. 5)

variation: the occurrence of different traits that make organisms different from each other within the same species (Ch. 6 and 8)

velocity: the speed an object is moving in a given direction (Ch. 3)

Venus: second planet from the sun in our Solar System (Ch. 11)

vernal equinox: the day in spring in which the length of the day is equal to the length of the night (Ch. 11)

vestigial structure: a bodily structure that once was useful to an organism but now no longer serves any purpose (Ch. 8)

volcanoes: weak spots in the crust of Earth where magma comes to the surface (Ch. 9)

volume: the amount of space taken up by an object (Ch. 2)

water cycle: the process through which water moves from bodies of water, land, and living things on Earth's surface into the atmosphere and then back down to Earth's surface (Ch. 7 and 10)

water vapor: water in its gaseous state (Ch. 10)

weathering: the process that breaks down rock and other substances on Earth's surface both physically and chemically (Ch. 9)

winter solstice: the shortest day of the year, usually December 21 in the northern hemisphere (Ch. 11)

work: the energy that is transferred through force and motion (Ch. 4)